The Crone's Book
of Charms & Spells

"It would be easy to imagine that this book was found in an old trunk in an attic, written lovingly by hand with herbs pressed between the pages."

—Ellen Cannon Reed
author of *The Witches Tarot*

"This little gem is a bridge between the Craft of the ancients and the needs of the modern Witch. A field guide to the lore and craft of magic."

—Anodea Judith
author of *Wheels of Life*

The Magical Crone 🌿

An ivy-covered cottage nestled in the forest…an old woman gathering herbs by the light of the moon…a cauldron hissing and bubbling with ancient magics. Walk up the path to the old wooden door and knock three times. The crone welcomes you to sit by her hearth and share the secrets of her magic.…

The Crone's Book of Charms & Spells holds the carefully guarded secrets that a Wise Woman of bygone days could have penned in her grimoire by candlelight. Herbal elixirs, powerful charms, amulets, balms for all folk who come to her seeking their heart's desire: healing, protection, love, fertility, wealth, marriage, youthfulness, beauty.

This quaint and mystic treasury of lore describes twelve rituals to guide you through the mysteries of a full year of seasons. Begin with an ice-sparkling ceremony for the first day of the year and celebrate the winter solstice in a glorious burst of red and gold fire. Each ceremony grows out of the unchanging truths of the cycle of seasons and of the universe itself.

Knock at the door of this little cottage. You'll uncover all the rich magic of a wise crone's book of lore.

About the Author 🌿

Valerie Worth was a prolific writer whose work included numerous books of children's poetry and fiction for both young people and adults. In 1991, the National Council of Teachers of English honored her with their Poetry Award for Excellence in Poetry for Children. Her poems are vivid observations of the quiet rumblings of everyday objects. In all her writing, the careful attention to rhythm and sound and her striking images and metaphors make for engaging reading.

Valerie Worth was born in Philadelphia, and as a child she lived in Pennsylvania, Florida and India. She attended Swarthmore College and graduated in 1955. Afterwards, she settled in Clinton, New York, and continued her writing. She had many other interests, including astronomy, gardening and meditation. Valerie Worth died in 1994. She is survived by her husband, George Bahlke, and three children.

A Note from George Bahlke 🌿

Valerie Worth wrote these spells out of her great interest in the history of magic and her love of poetry. In rereading them, I have admired their powerful evocation of the spirit inherent in all occult wisdom. At the same time, readers should be aware that some of the charms, among them "A Charm to Work Revenge," "A Charm to Win Control Over Another," "A Charm to Waste Another's Wealth," and "A Charm to Bind an Enemy," are imitations of older magic; they were composed to be read, not practiced. Valerie would have been distressed if any of these charms were to bring harm to anyone; indeed, she thought poetry and magic should bring us joy and a sense of celebration. For her poetry itself was a ritual, a ritual she endeavored to express adequately and appropriately to the subject of the charm or poem she was working on.

The Crone's Book
of Charms
& Spells

Valerie Worth

1999
Llewellyn Publications
St. Paul, Minnesota 55164-0383, U.S.A.

SECOND EDITION
Third printing, 1999
(Previously titled *The Crone's Book of Wisdom*)
First Edition published by Llewellyn Publications, 1988

Cover art and design: Lisa Novak and Anne Marie Garrison
Cover photo: Leo Tushaus
Interior talisman art: Anne Marie Garrison
Interior design and layout: Virginia Sutton
Project management: Kimberly Nightingale
Interior spot illustrations from public domain sources, many courtesy of Dover Publications.

Library of Congress Cataloguing in Publication Data
Worth, Valerie.
        The crone's book of charms & spells / Valerie Worth. — 2nd ed.
                p. cm.
        Rev. ed. of: The crone's book of wisdom. 1st ed. 1988.
        ISBN 1-56718-811-7 (pbk.)
        1. Herbs—Folklore.   2. Charms.   3. Incantations.   I. Title.
    GR780.W68   1998
    398'.3--dc21   97-52251
                                                                CIP

Publisher's Note:
Llewellyn Worldwide does not participate in, endorse, or have any authority or responsibility concerning private business transactions between our authors and the public. All mail addressed to the author is forwarded but the publisher cannot, unless specifically instructed by the author, give out an address or phone number.

Llewellyn Publications
A Division of Llewellyn Worldwide, Ltd.
P.O. Box 64383, Dept. K811-7
St. Paul, MN 55164-0383

Printed in the United States of America

Other Books by Valerie Worth 🌿

The Crone's Book of Words, 1971
    (Llewellyn Publications)
Small Poems, 1972 (Farrar, Straus & Giroux)
More Small Poems, 1976 (Farrar, Straus & Giroux)
Still More Small Poems, 1978
    (Farrar, Straus & Giroux)
Curliques: The Fortunes of Two Pug Dogs, 1980
    (Farrar, Straus & Giroux)
Gypsy Gold, 1983 (Farrar, Straus & Giroux)
Fox Hill, 1986 (Farrar, Straus & Giroux)
Small Poems Again, 1986 (Farrar, Straus & Giroux)
All the Small Poems, 1987 (Farrar, Straus & Giroux)
At Christmas Time, 1992 (Harper Collins)
All the Small Poems and Fourteen More, 1994
    (Farrar, Straus & Giroux)

Contents

Introduction

Of the Pleasures and Virtues in These Works 🌿

THIS BOOK CONTAINS much matter concerning what may well be done, from day to day, in the practice of the magical arts, not only such high activity of spirit as shall inspire and enlighten, but also certain ways in which the hands may work to create from earthly substance a fair array of objects and inventions, both immediately useful and potentially of vast power. There is pleasure in the fashioning of these things, and pleasure also in their further employment. Sprung in simple form from the hands, they return great nourishment to the spirit, being both well made and well conceived.

Such entities as herb brews, potions, oils, charms, candles, amulets, robes, etc., shall act well in themselves to please and serve. Yet also, when they are incorporated into larger acts of the imagination, as in certain arcane cere-monies ultimately to be described, it shall be seen that all the spirit's wisdom may be made manifest by the artful use of these materials.

Thus the virtues of Great Wisdom may enlighten the hands as readily as the spirit, and when hands and spirit are instructed and prepared they may act as one to raise from humble works a larger realm of magic—minor artifacts transformed into symbols of universal meaning, based ever upon the homeliest of recipes—whereby an herb may grow to touch the very Sun, or a single candle light the dead back into the living cosmos.

The Materials of Wisdom

HERE SHALL BE told the method and the substance, the means and requirements, for certain arts of benefit to both the body and the mind, used ordinarily and daily, yet also in rites and observations of an elevated nature. If these instructions are attended and remembered, the practices envisioned further in this book shall be assumed with greater ease and clarity.

Herb Brews

It is better that the herbs from our gardens or the wild woods and fields be taken in this way—drunk fresh in all their strength—than wasted and weakened in flavorings for victuals, thus to comfort only the vain palate. These brews are true powers, whereas the same herbs cooked in food are poor wraiths of themselves. Honor them as they deserve, and they shall not fail.

The fair leaves or other necessary parts should be gathered as young and fair as possible, and a handful placed in a plain brown teapot of good size. Fill the pot then with fresh-boiling water, and allow this tea to steep for twelve minutes by the hourglass or clock. Pour it out then straightaway into a cup; sweeten it with a teaspoonful of honey, and drink the infusion while it is hot.

A few of the well-known herbs that may be used for such purposes follow here:

❧ **Anise, the Amorous:** The seeds, to strengthen passions

❧ **Basil, the Courageous:** Against faintness of heart

❧ **Borage, the Inspiring:** Against aches in the limbs

🌿 **Caraway, the Sweet:** The seeds, for mental vigor

🌿 **Catnip, the Subtle:** Against fever and chills

🌿 **Mint, the Comforting:** Against afflictions of the stomach

🌿 **Nasturtium, the Pungent:** Against the headache

🌿 **Parsley, the Stout:** Against pallor and frailty

🌿 **Red Clover, the Succulent:** The flowers, for good temper

🌿 **Rosemary, the Fair:** To soothe the nerves

🌿 **Rue, the Mysterious:** To assuage guilt and sorrow

🌿 **Sage, the Powerful:** Against melancholy and distress of the mind

🌿 **Thyme, the Sovereign:** Against coughs

🌿 **White Pine, the Healthful:** Against colds and catarrh

🌿 **Wild Ginger, the Profound:** The root, against lassitude

An Elixir of Honey 🌿

To strengthen the constitution and dispel afflictions of the mind and body, this honey elixir has no equal. It is pure and wholesome, and may be taken as a tonic by children, grown men and women, and ancients alike, with good results. Concoct it thus:

❦ Boil in eight ounces of water the fresh leaves of sage, thyme, and mint, a large spoonful of each, until of liquid there be left but an ounce or two. Pour off this brew, and when it is cool add to it a teaspoonful of good brown cider vinegar, and also three ounces of honey, strained fresh from the comb. Stir these well until the honey is blended and the whole shines clear. Then it may be sipped, from a wine glass, all or in part. If any is not used, it may be kept in a tightly corked vessel for later draughts.

On Using Wild Herbs for 🌿 Practical and Magical Purposes

Certain plants of the commonest sort may be of great use in the procuring of both physical and spiritual benefits. It would be superfluous to treat at length here those cultivated herbs all gardeners know, powerful though they be for tonics and teas; yet those other plants, the lowly stalks many ignore by the path or roadside, or from which they idly strip the leaves with no thought of what treasures they cast down, may serve the Wise most faithfully.

Cherish then those leaves, flowers, or other parts that are healthful, and pluck them at their height, to be dried and brewed as teas, or otherwise used as will be directed. Those that are of value in their spiritual aspects may be prepared and duly fashioned into charms, and kept carefully, as will be described.

Here follow some whose virtues are undeniable, yet too little honored by most persons (who surely ever have need of them).

❧ The yellow **Avens,** called also Geum, has a modest flower which yet produces pertinacious hooked seeds. Take then its manner as a pattern, and bind twenty-two of these seeds in a small bag of gauze, to call forth strength of purpose from even the most malleable of natures.

❧ The leaves of the **Bayberry** will produce a vigorous tea, of healthful flavor and inspiriting vapor, good to be taken by those who require renewal in the midst of misfortune. The silver frosted

BAYBERRY

berries may be boiled a while in rainwater and the freed wax then skimmed off the surface. This wax mixed with a pure oil will make a balm of value for soothing the skin, and hence the mind.

🌱 **Bedstraw,** its stalks starred along their length by radiating leaves, should be laid beneath the pillow, secretly, to strengthen a failing marriage.

🌱 The **Bindweed,** unwrapped from some other plant to which it clings, may be thrice knotted and thus kept to assure the fidelity of a lover. If it should break at all in the knotting, it must be cast away and another strand of the weed gathered. Yet if three strands should thus break, it shall be a sign that this lover is weak and unworthy of your attentions.

BEDSTRAW

🌱 The **Black Mustard,** a plant of great vigor, may be dried and worn in a bag about the neck for safety from illness and misadventure. It shall also be of value when held in the hand during an eclipse of the Sun, assuring that no evil influence may enter into one upon whom the Moon's shadow falls.

🌱 Burrs of the **Burdock,** packed in a wooden box, must inspire honesty in one to whom they are given. There is also another use that shall be shown later in this book.

🌿 The **Buttercup,** its blossoms filled to overflowing with the Sun's benisons, shall confer a harmony as of milk and honey upon the household where a bunch is hung over the doorway, and the falling petals allowed to remain for a week upon the threshold.

🌿 Use the golden sap of the **Celandine** as a powerful ink, especially for charmed inscriptions upon parchment or fine leather.

🌿 The lowly **Chickweed,** flowering like small stars tangled in the meadow grasses, may yield a tea of noble nourishment; also let it be wound into a garland and hung about the neck to attract the favors of the Heavens.

🌿 Cut ten strong stalks of blue-flowered **Chicory** with a sharp knife and bind them about from top to bottom with a cord. This wand should then be given to one who is ill that he may be strengthened in blood, flesh, and bone.

🌿 All **Cinquefoils** assist the works of magic. Sprigs thick-leaved should be held in the hand for some moments before the inception of any spiritual task, and likewise after such an undertaking is completed.

CINQUEFOIL

DAISY

❧ The **Daisy** is named Flower of the White Sun, and all endeavors of high virtue may be better accomplished by its influence. Where this plant blooms, you shall walk about it thrice and name it as it is named here. Take away a single flower, from which the petals should then be plucked and pressed in a white paper. Thereafter swallow one petal each day, again naming the name, until all shall be consumed and your own pure fire thereby strengthened.

❧ Collect some white sap from stalks of the **Dandelion**, and mix it with a little cow's milk as a bitter potion—this to be performed and taken when you would chasten greed and pride, lest these faults lead you from the ways of truth.

❧ The **Fringed Loosestrife** shall yield inner peace to one who gathers it from the roadside and wears it on the breast for seven days.

❧ **Goatsbeard,** combining powers of the Sun and Moon, as its head is first gold-rayed and then silverglobed, should be plucked in both guises and the stems' juices pressed upon your palms. Thus shall the right hand and the left hand both serve you well.

🌿 **Ground Ivy,** called also Gill-over-the-Ground, may be brewed into a bitter tea and sipped, to overcome weakness and timidity. Strewn about the floors of the house, these leaves will promote serenity and benign dreams.

GROUND IVY

🌿 The **Heal-All,** also called Self-Heal, is in all its parts most fervent as a favorable charm. Dried, tied up in a bag of purple silk and hung on a cord about the neck, it will soothe the stomach, clear the consciousness, enliven the eye, and guard the hand from hesitation. Treat this good herb with esteem and it shall not fail.

🌿 The **Jewelweed,** also called Touch-Me-Not, and also Orange Balsam, provides a most excellent lotion for afflictions of the skin, particularly ivy poisoning. Crush the whole plant and press its juices upon the malady, then bind on a good number of the leaves, bruised, as a poultice. This should be left in place from dawn to dawn.

🌿 Beware the powerful **Jimsonweed,** an ancient poison. Shun its touch, yet wearing a glove uproot it and carry it to the rat's tunnel. Forthwith thrust it in, and drive it deep below with an iron rod or stake. This should then be repeated with further stalks until the space is filled, which will thus be of great efficacy in driving away the thieving vermin.

JUNIPER

❧ Take berried branches of the **Juniper** at the Winter Solstice and hang them over your doorway for thirteen days. Then take them down and pluck the berries therefrom, saving these in a small box, in honor of life renewed. Keep them well all the year, until the Winter Solstice comes again, when they should be solemnly burned and the same gathering of branches performed anew.

❧ The elegant **Lady's Thumb,** as it grows perfect and chaste in the worst of waste places, shall be plucked and kept for a charm against all foulness and corruption.

❧ **Lady's Sorrel,** called also Sourgrass, may well be eaten as it grows, for health and a clear intelligence, or else be brewed into a broth, with a little salt added, to the same end.

❧ The **May Apple,** called also False Mandrake, may be used for the same purposes of sorcery as the true and deadly Mandrake or Mandragora. While its fruit is benign, it serves also magically, whereby it should be dried and pierced with spines of the Hawthorn as an object of spite. The root is a source of poison, and may be employed in a dire charm later prescribed within this book.

᠅ The fragrant **Melilot**, called also Sweet Clover, both white and yellow varieties, should be gathered in great bunches when it flowers, and hung upon the walls of every chamber in your house. Thus will its scent prove a benison to you for many months thereafter.

᠅ When the **Milkweed** buds and blooms along the dusty roadside, its emanations are as of the costliest perfume; yet who, passing by, shall think to savor it? Gather then an immense bouquet, and set it soon in water within your house. This attention shall be rewarded by such sweetening of the air that all evil shall be driven from your spirit, and you shall be thus blessed as long as the fragrance shall last.

᠅ The clever **Mistletoe**, of berries white and leaves substantial, shall render powerless your staunchest enemy if you will keep it hung above your bed; and later in this book a further charm shall yet be told.

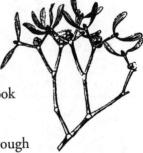

MISTLETOE

᠅ A stiff sprig of **Motherwort**, rough with leaves, ripe-seeded and sharp- husked, should be carried to the place where a

woman lies in labor. Its keen barbs are scratched lightly upon each of her palms; two leaves are laid upon her brow, and a leaf given her in either hand to grasp. Thus shall she be succored by the Earth, who stands Midwife of midwives to all life.

❧ Pound well in a mortar the fresh leaves of **Mullein,** and make of them a poultice for infections, warts, and rashes of the skin. These woolly leaves, whole, may be used in charms attracting fertility and prosperity to those whose lands grow dry and barren.

❧ A few seeds of **Peppergrass** should be chewed to cure the headache. They may also be used as a charm for wealth.

❧ Pluck up the lowly **Pineapple Weed** by its poor roots, and crush it in the hands; such fruitful fragrance shall thereby be liberated as shall renew forgotten hope and expectation, and inspire the hands to strengthened works.

❧ The **Plantain** of common growth, its hardy spike arising from broad leaves, shall, when decocted to a lotion with rain water, and rubbed upon the skin, invigorate the whole flesh to a condition of redemption, and the senses to a state of exhaltation.

PLANTAIN

🌿 Gather the spiked leaves of **Prickly Lettuce** and dry them well, then crush them, and they may be burned as an incense to renew the senses and heal the wounded spirit.

🌿 Brew the young leaves of **Queen Anne's Lace** (taking care that it be indeed this herb itself, and not one of those, as the notorious Hemlock, that resembles it but yields an extreme poison) and thus produce a tea of very healthful flavor and properties. The petals of the dried blossoms, scattered throughout the house, shall work a beneficial influence on all who live therein.

🌿 Those who suffer in summer from the pollen of **Ragweed** should take the plant before it flowers, break it small, and pound these fragments to a dust. A pinch of this powder placed, on each of seven mornings, upon the left palm, while the word *laedo* is uttered, shall serve to weaken the plant's powers over the afflicted.

RAGWEED

🌿 **St. Johnswort,** an herb of ancient repute, may simply be carried in the pocket as a powerful charm against all evil. Otherwise it is useful as a beneficial bath, if the leaves and flowers are infused in a tubful of water and the whole body immersed therein.

❧ The **Sandbur,** called also Sand Spur, whose hurtful spines will sting the careless foot, may yet bring an assuagement of pain to the grieving and heartsore. Wrap three of these burrs in a lock of lamb's wool and keep these in a small bag of leather hung about the neck, for the length of three lunar months. So shall the viper sorrow be vanquished.

❧ Scrub the teeth with a split twig of **Sassafras** for cleanliness of the mouth and facility of speech. Flatten three of its lobed leaves within a book, and later hang them in your window against the works of evil wizards; boil its twigs in water to produce a lotion of benefit to the skin. In all ways this plant shall be of service to you and further your well-being.

SASSAFRAS

❧ The **Stinging Nettle,** which must in wisdom be avoided for its malevolent properties, yet shall yield a nutritious tea if the leaves are plucked young (by hands safeguarded in gloves the while). Also it may work a fitting revenge upon one who has betrayed you, if a box full of the stems, these wrapped in gaudy paper, be sent to the offender secretly at the waxing of the Moon.

🌿 The **Sunflower,** whether growing wild or boldly planted in the garden, may bestow great strength upon all who attend it. Let one plant be observed from day to day, and when its fire shall cool, its growth cease, and its seed be firm, cut the bowed head off with a hand's length of stalk remaining. Tie this tightly with a cord, and thus suspend it from a hook fixed to a ceiling within your house, that it may hang there all the winter and be well preserved. In the spring take it down, remove the seeds, and plant all but one of these in a great circle surrounding your house. The remaining seed you should then crack open and swallow the kernel thereof, thus to become one with its Sun-engendered flesh, while you live thereafter encircled by the new flowers that grow— yourself the fertile center of their solar influence.

🌿 The purple blooming **Thistle,** of many forms and sizes, is, like the Stinging Nettle, both vicious and mild. For its best use, take from it the sword-guarded flowers, when in the autumn they shall pale and open to silver silk. Collect this fine floss, and pack it into a small box, to be kept in readiness thereafter to treat any

THISTLE

bleeding wound. Lay it soon, in abundance, upon the place, saying:

> *Thistledown across thee*
> *Now comfort, stanch, and close thee.*

VIOLET

🌿 The **Violet,** herb of beauty and true love, yields a tea of exquisite azure if the flowers be duly steeped in boiling water. This identical infusion is also to be used in preparing a ceremonial potion which will later in this book be described. Presently the recipe will be given for a charmed confection made from Violet blossoms.

🌿 Behold the motley **Viper's Bugloss,** of spired flowers fair to view yet frail, of spiny stems and leaves all pricking and bristling. One blossom from each of seven stalks, to be plucked and pressed dry within a sacred book, then kept in a folded paper over the heart, shall strengthen the immortal spirit.

🌿 The **Wild Rose** embodies such immutable sweetness and immaculate virtue that a tea made from its petals and given to any malefactor must change his very nature.

❧ Likewise a dust of rose petals, well dried, pulverized, and mixed with a little powdered **Orrisroot,** may be sprinkled in the bed of a contrary lover; so shall it turn love's vagaries to a faithful path again.

❧ The **Woody Nightshade,** also called Bittersweet, has not the deadly character of the greater nightshades. Yet take it not for brew or potion, lest its kinship with these others work you harm. Use it, rather, for the comely and passionate appearance of its flowers and berries, as a charmed bouquet, to bestow where you would receive in return the amorous desires of a lover.

❧ Leaves of the melancholy scented bone-pale **Yarrow** may serve as an aromatic to revive the fainting senses, or as a tea to slake the thirst of a fevered brain, but best of all as a reminder of mortality. Dried and hung up above the mirror where you most often see your face, it shall remain a chastisement to all ambitious vanities.

Yet as Moon without Sun loses her strength, so yarrow's truth is incomplete.

❧ For the whole of wisdom, you must match it with the solar **Goldenrod,** gathering both at their height. Set them to dry within an earthen jar, to bloom and shine all winter, and favor you with signs of everlasting life. Thereby shall you be made all-wise, seeing that death, while potent, is not omnipotent.

The Creation of Charms ❦

While the foregoing recipes for simple charms have taken
sundry herbs as their basis, nearly any object may be used
for such purposes if it be fitting in significance, duly prepared, and properly kept. Whether it be an herb, a pebble,
a bone, a curl of dust, a pinch of Earth, a gem, an inscribed
paper, or anything chosen cleverly to serve the desired
intention, its power will lie as much in the inspiring properties which the object itself possesses, as in its ritual dedication. Thus while certain ancient and traditional charms
may always be recommended, as particularly suited to certain needs, yet new ones may still be invented if the corre-
spondence between object and necessity is imaginatively
appropriate.

❧ For a charm of high power and complexity it is best
that a ritual incantation first be spoken over the object (or
compatible combination of several objects) to release and
direct its powers toward the realm in which they shall oper-
ate; then it may be anointed, or combined with some oil or
balm of suitable scent, in a place of silence and secrecy,
embellished by the presence of burning candles or an
incense. Finally, the object (or objects) may be sewn up in a
bag of cloth, or a small leather pouch, to be carried on the
person, or worn about the neck, or hidden somewhere in
safety; it may also be well guarded in a small wooden box
upon which some further inscription has been set.

🌿 Any words originally spoken for the charm's dedication may be inscribed upon it, or repeated daily over it, thus strengthening its influence and the intention of its bearer. It should never be lost or forgotten, lest such neglect turn its powers awry; but if it be no longer needed, it should be carefully burned or buried with some fitting words of dismissal.

A later portion of this book will describe a number of highly elaborate and efficacious charms, their ingredients, mode of preparation, appropriate incantations, and all influences and circumstances under which they should be created.

The Creation of Talismans 🌿

The talismans envisioned in this book work much in the manner of charms, save that they bear certain specific inscriptions in which their power principally lies, the objects themselves being of less obvious significance. Thus a common pebble or small stone, of texture and form allowing the surface to be sufficiently inscribed, serves as well as any thing, and is easily discovered in the garden or even on the roadside.

Such a stone should be well scrubbed with soap and water and dried completely. It may be covered with a white paint or left to its natural surface, upon which the inscription is set, either incised with a sharp instrument, or applied with colored paints if there be a symbolic design or picture, or with India ink where words are used. Generally both design and words together will serve with the best effect. The stone may be chosen for the value of its natural configuration, such as one of heart shape for a talisman pertaining to love, a crescent for some lunar influence, circular for the Sun, etc. When the talisman is completed, it should be ritually dedicated and preserved in the same fashion as a charm.

Further in this book will be found a collection of inscriptions, both verbal and pictorial, appropriate to such talismans.

Amulets and Magical Rings ❧

An inscribed amulet is best worn about the neck (although some few are suited to the wrist or ankle) attached to a woven cord, a chain, or a leather thong. Thus a small medal or pendant, cut from some firm metal as copper or silver, will serve admirably. It will be ornamental, and is often

worn openly, rather than hidden as would be a talisman or charm. However, any words in its inscription should be placed on the reverse side, worn next to the body, and only some symbolic design or image displayed upon the outward face. Thus a certain degree of secrecy will still be preserved; and when these words are written in the ancient Latin tongue, an even stronger obscurity will guard their purpose and protect their powers from dissipation.

An amulet of this nature is often used to celebrate some truth, or to affirm some belief, or to express some aspiration; it is seldom appropriate to the darker purposes —active revenge or malefaction (for these, a charm is always best suited). For example, to honor the Sun, to deny the power of death, to seek wisdom, to win love; all such are suited to the fair nature of these magical adornments.

❧ In the matter of rings as well, any words should be inscribed on the inner surface thereof, with images upon the outward and visible side. A simple ring cut from a strip of metal, smoothed and shaped to a circle, is excellent for this

purpose, and since it is worn openly, may also be given a highly decorative appearance.

❧ Amulets and rings of metal may be engraved, or they may be inscribed with paints and India ink in the same way as stone talismans. In this case, a protective lacquer should be applied over all to keep the inscription from wearing away.

When they are well fashioned and adapted to the nature of the ritual, these amulets and rings are worn to great advantage on ceremonial occasions. Before such use, and even for less formal purposes, they may be dedicated and anointed in the same way as charms and talismans.

A number of appropriate inscriptions for amulets and rings will be given later in this book.

Scented Oils 🌿

All perfumes are of profound importance in directing the senses and the imagination toward specific ends. Every scent possesses its own character, and should not be used carelessly. Rather, it should be chosen scrupulously for its effect upon the occasion and the wearer. Cleverly used, a perfume will provide a powerful influence on the circumstances surrounding its application, whether to a person or an object.

🌿 To prepare a pure and delicate scent, take some clear, light, odorless oil—one ounce—and warm it over the fire for six minutes, along with a large spoonful of aromatic woods, or roots, fragrant leaves or flowers (all first well dried, then crushed or pounded in a mortar). Let this mixture cool, then pour it out, to steep within a jar well sealed for twelve days thereafter. On the thirteenth day, strain it  through fine cloth into a small basin; thence funnel it into a vial and stop it tight. If this preparation should not yield a strong enough perfume, as some occasions demand greater sharpness or pungency, certain essences of a less subtle nature may be bought and added to the original infusion— yet take care that such combinations be compatible, lest the pure character of the scent be sacrificed.

Such an oil may serve for anointments of the skin, either for ceremony, or for improved health, or simply for adornment. It may anoint candles to give them fragrance, or charms and other magical objects to consecrate them. It may also be mixed into tinctures and balms, or with liquid wax when a new candle is being molded.

Each of the ceremonies presented later in this book requires the use of a specific scent in some form for its

symbolic embellishment. When such a ritual is actually practiced, the efficacy of these perfumes becomes most evident.

Fragrant Tinctures ❧

❧ Take nearly three ounces of a strong, unscented alcohol
and add to it whatever fragrant matter is chosen, whether
leaves, roots, or flowers, thoroughly dried and crushed, or
else some previously prepared scented oil, ten or twelve
drops (or more, if the oil be faint). Shake these together
well, and let stand twelve days, after which the tincture may
be strained clear through a cloth.

   Used for refreshment of the face and body, particularly before any ceremony, such a tincture will inspire the
thoughts to strength, and the occasion to good issue.

The Preparation of Balms ❧

❧ Melt together, over a low fire, pure
beeswax and an oil of coconut, olive, or
some other benign vegetable, one ounce
of each. Add a few fragments of dyed
candle wax if any color should be
required, and twelve drops of strong-
scented oil. Warm all of these until they
are well mixed; then pour them out into a
small jar or seamless box.

A balm so prepared shall be of great power in ceremonial anointments of the brow, throat, wrists, etc., either before or during the celebration (as may be learned later in this book). The face shall be made fair, the hands strengthened, and the body enlivened by such application, as also any ritual object may be better consecrated if the proper scent be spread upon it. Yet take care that the scent be fitting to the use, one that is warm and sweet for purposes connected with the Sun, cool and sharp for the Moon, dark and heavy for night, or secrecy, and strong and pungent for Earth, new life, etc.

There are also healing properties to a balm of fine substance and fragrance, and for all aches of the body and brain, great comfort can be found in such anointment.

Candles and Incenses ❦

Excellent candles may be made thus: melt beeswax, or paraffin wax, or the wax of Bayberries, over a very low heat. Then stir in a spoonful of some fragrant oil, color the candle as required by adding shavings of drawing wax, and when all these substances are clear and well blended, pour them into a small earthenware vessel, with a depth of two or three inches. This vessel may be made especially for the purpose out of garden clay, and inscribed before it is dry with a sharp knife or twig. Before the wax is poured, a length of sturdy string should be tied to a rod or stick placed across the vessel's rim, so that the string runs straight down through its center. Then pour in the wax, and set the vessel aside for an hour or so, after which the rod may be removed and the wick cut to a proper length.

Long tapers may be bought and used for ritual purposes, but their colors must be carefully chosen never too pale or too harsh, and always befitting the ceremonial occasion. They should be anointed with fragrant oils to give them power and spirit, either by hand or by using a small brush of camel's hair.

An incense may be created from any pungent or sweet scented leaves, flowers, or roots, by drying these thoroughly and grinding them to powder in a mortar. Perfumed oils are often added to give strength to this substance. Then it may be burnt in a small brass bowl, or scattered upon glowing coals in a heavy iron cauldron. The rising smoke from this or any incense is of great benefit to all ceremonial occasions, as a symbol of spiritual ascent as well as an inspiration to the senses.

Ceremonial Potions or Libations ❦

During certain rituals, or for other specific purposes or occasions, these spirituous mixtures are offered to good effect. They may represent an abstract quality, or inspire the mind to some significant awareness, or soothe the body to a state of well-being, according to their concoction and the circumstances of their being taken. Here follow several, of readily procurable components, all first to be well blended

before pouring out into some ceremonial goblet or chalice:

❧ One ounce of brandy, two
ounces of sweet white port, one teaspoonful of honey—an excellent
libation in rituals of solar import.

❧ Two ounces of anise cordial,
one ounce of Russian vodka, one
teaspoonful of white corn syrup—
for lunar rites, unsurpassed.

❧ One ounce of cherry brandy, one ounce of peach
brandy, one teaspoonful of honey, a sprinkling of cumin
powder—for inspiring love or passion.

❧ One ounce of green mint cordial, two ounces of white
gin, one teaspoonful of white corn syrup—for renewed
vision and intellect.

❧ One ounce of apricot brandy, two ounces of sweet
Madeira wine, three drops of almond extract—for beauty of
mind and body.

❧ One ounce of blackberry brandy, one ounce of sweet
red port, one-half teaspoonful of vanilla—for triumph over
death.

❧ One ounce of apple brandy, two ounces of apple cider,
one teaspoonful of honey—for improved health.

These potions are of great strength, and should be offered with restraint, lest they overwhelm the sensibilities and lead only to a confusion of their original purposes.

Ceremonial Robes, Shawls, Scarves, Etc. ❦

To surround the body with symbolic beauty is the prime purpose of ceremonial garments. Thus, such clothing should not obscure the flesh, but act as its fitting enhancement and adornment. Choose, therefore, first a soft and close-fitting tunic and hose, or other like garments, dyed to an appropriate color (black may often be used for its neutrality, its suggestion of secrecy, and its harmony with nocturnal rituals) to cover yet to well reveal the limbs and the bodily form.

Above these, next, various robes, or shawls, or veils, or long scarves, of a soft, thin, even transparent nature should be worn, to spread an ethereal film upon the fleshly contour of the costume. These floating garments may envelop the body from neck to ankle, or cover only the back and shoulders, or even, as with scarves, trail free, attached only at the neck or waist or wrists, but all should be flowing and fine, of fitting color, and sometimes bearing a design or inscription related to the ceremony for which they are worn.

🌿 Thus for rituals pertaining to the Sun, there may be small figures of solar import, either words or signs, embroidered in gold thread or inscribed with a gold paint, upon the borders of the robe, with perhaps a gold Sun represented on the breast. On scarves and shawls also, the borders may be adorned in this fashion, and a significant symbol marked in the center of the cloth.

🌿 Scarves should be narrow, the length six times the width, shawls triangular, and large enough to cover the upper arms as well as the back, though they may be worn covering the hair as well. A robe is easily made from two lengths of cloth hemmed at the ends, having a width of four feet, and long enough to reach from shoulder to ankle, sewn together up each side to within eight inches or so of the top, and then joined all across the top save for an opening large enough for the head to pass through. This robe will serve for woman or man, being entirely neutral in design. Yet take care that these thin materials be kept far from the candle flame, lest they take fire and cause their wearer some injury.

Clothing of this sort should be carefully folded and stored away in a chest or box strewn with aromatics such as lavender or shaved orrisroot, that they may keep their power, and endure, and serve you well. Be instructed here that the garments described for certain ceremonies treated later in this book are all conceived according to these directions.

Inscriptions
of Power

As words embrace all things, seen and unseen, so these inscriptions hold within their bounds the essences of what they name. What is invoked exists within its invocation; what is set down is brought to bear on all it touches and on all that surrounds it.

Do not discount the power of such words, or of the signs and images that well attend them, for they are rich with the wisdom of centuries, and in both ancient and immediate guises they may raise the spirits of their origins, the forces that created them, the world of revelation in which they were conceived.

Thus to call upon the sources whence they have sprung is to summon the strength of their creators' visionary minds, yet people whose ways were closer to the ways of Earth than ours may be again. The names and images these ancients wrought, for the same elements and entities we still must fashion into life, are potent indeed; and we do well to set them down upon those objects we desire to hallow and empower. As even now we shape words to our purposes, so do these words continue to shape the working of the Cosmos.

The Inscription of Talismans 🌱

The words and images that follow may be set upon various objects presenting themselves to the imagination as appropriate for use as talismans, whether smooth and shapely stones or rocks, blocks, or chips of fine-grained wood, polished metal disks, leaves of venerable parchment, leather trimmed and burnished, and the like. These objects should be so chosen as to provide two faces. The first, or upper, is to be inscribed primarily with emblems, symbols, or images; the second, or reverse, should bear the words themselves, as convenants and invocations. Such talismans may be displayed openly, yet they are most often kept in secrecy, according to their purpose and appearance. If they are small, they may be carried upon the person to good effect. Here follow then, certain inscriptions most fit for their empowering:

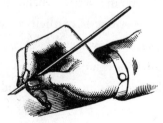

✤ For Beauty

Upon the first face of the talisman
shall be depicted a small disk
with five rays, as a star, flanked
by the crescent Moon and fiery
Sun. Upon the reverse shall be
written, in characters well formed,
these words:

> *Morning star*
> *And evening star*
> *By thy light*
> *I grow fair.*

✤ For Dividing Lovers

Upon one face, the crescent Moon
enclosing the image of a skull.
Upon the reverse, these words:

> *This love*
> *The moon*
> *Doth shrink*
> *To bone.*

❧ Against All Sorrow

Upon one face, the headstone of a grave, bearing a skull. Upon the reverse, these words:

> *Sorrow be dust and dust*
> *dissolve:*
> *Let all my grief go into this grave.*

❧ To Gain Wealth

Upon one face, the full rayed Sun enclosing a crescent Moon and three stars. Upon the reverse, these words:

> *Yet earthly gold*
> *I soon shall hold.*

❧ For Stability

Upon one face, a skull from which issue the eight legs of a spider, set at the center of a web. Upon the reverse, these words:

> *My threads bind*
> *The restless mind*

❧ For Eternal Youth

Upon one face, the many-rayed disk of the Sun. Upon the reverse, these words:

> *Who bear my gold*
> *Ne'er grows old.*

❧ For Good Fortune

Upon one face, a fair fish curled about the globe of the Earth. Upon the reverse, these words:

> *Flowering earth*
> *Flowing sea*
> *Fatten, fill,*
> *And favor me.*

❧ To Win Healing from the Sun

Upon one face, the disk of the Sun, full rayed. Upon the reverse, these words:

> *My orb and rays*
> *Grant thee ease.*

🐝 To Be Given to Another, for Love

Upon one face, a heart from which flames radiate as from the Sun. Upon the reverse, these words:

> *My fire thine*
> *Thy heart mine.*

🐝 For Rebirth of the Spirit

Upon one face, a seed of the sunflower, contained within curved stem, leaves, and blossom of this plant. Upon the reverse, these words:

> *Old seed, new flower,*
> *I bear thy power.*

🐝 For Relief from Pain

Upon one face, an eye, rayed with flames as the Sun. Upon the reverse, these words:

> *Who meets my eye*
> *His pain must fly.*

❧ For Good Health

Upon one face, a hand from whose fingertips spring flames, as from candles. Upon the reverse, these words:

> *Who holds my hand*
> *May health command.*

❧ To Overcome the Season of Winter

Upon one face, the Sun rayed with alternate flames and leaves. Upon the reverse, these words:

> *Poor sun, forlorn in winter's*
> *grave*
> *Arise and burn that all may live.*

❧ Against Falsehood and Deception

Upon one face, a serpent curled head to tail, encircling an eye rayed with flames. Upon the reverse, these words:

> *The serpent wise*
> *Deals death to lies.*

❦ For Warmth and Well-Being in Winter

Upon one face, the head of a fox rayed with flames. Upon the reverse, these words:

> *Now these together run red:*
> *Man, fire, fox, sun, blood.*

❦ Against Melancholy

Upon one face, wreathed stalks and leaves of the herb Sage. Upon the reverse, these words:

> *Of fresh sage one gill*
> *Brewed in water*
> *Cures my ill.*

❦ For Immortality

Upon one face, stalks of grass that shed seeds rayed as Suns. Upon the reverse, these words:

> *Stalks brown*
> *Leaves old*
> *My seeds*
> *Bear gold.*

❧ For Loss of Weight

Upon one face, the Full Moon
flanked by crescent Moons.
Upon the reverse, these words:

> *Wax thou moon*
> *That I may wane;*
> *What I lose*
> *Then shalt thou gain.*

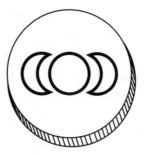

❧ For Fertility

Upon one face, an oval egg
containing the Sun rayed with
flames. Upon the reverse, these
words:

> *Earth and flesh now one*
> *In this egg, the sun.*

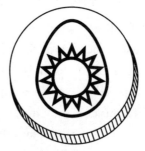

❧ Against Earthquakes

Upon one face, a stout vine encircling the globe of the Earth.
Upon the reverse, these words:

> *Now earth be fixed*
> *And dare not quake*
> *That I and mine*
> *May sleep and wake.*

🦎 For Safety in Traveling by Boat

Upon one face, a scallop shell encircled by waves of water. Upon the reverse, these words:

> *Earth and water bear thee*
> *Earth and water spare thee.*

The Inscription of Amulets 🦎

While any amulet may well be worn concealed, the ones recommended in this book are often worn openly, in the manner of decorative necklaces. Having their surfaces exposed to view, they require greater obscurity of language. To this end, only the Latin tongue is used for the words of these inscriptions, and thus a double benefit is obtained— both secrecy, and the tradition of an ancient language in which the words themselves recall elder sources of mystery and power.

As in the inscription of talismans, the first (and outer) face should bear the symbol or image, and the reverse all actual words.

Here, then, follow various inscriptions of power for such amulets as have been described earlier in this book (many of them are well suited to certain ceremonial occasions of which more shall be written anon):

🌺 To Honor the Sun

Upon one face, the Sun rayed with flames, its disk numbered as a sundial and containing a central gnomon. Upon the reverse, these words:

> *Sol cum homine ligo*
> *Uterque caecus solus*

🌺 For an Invocation of the Moon

Upon one face, the crescent Moon featured as in the human profile. Upon the reverse, these words:

> *Speculum meum*
> *Facies hominis*

🌺 To Discover the Philosopher's Stone

Upon one face, a Radiant Sun, about whose circumference these words are inscribed:

> *Nibredo albedo rubedo*

Upon the reverse, these words:

> *Cummutatis evenit*
> *Aurum soliferum*
> *Chrysos chrysos*

❧ To Win Love

Upon one face, a winged heart.
Upon the reverse, these words:

> *Amor*
> *Veni*
> *Cito*

❧ Another, for the Same

Upon one face, an open hand
with a heart set upon the palm.
Upon the reverse, these words:

> *Amor*
> *Te*
> *Teneo*

❧ To Inspire Passion

Upon one face, the Sun in
flames, enclosing a heart. Upon
the reverse, these words:

> *Amor te accendo:*
> *Do tibi solem*

❧ Against Sorrow

Upon one face, a bird, as the
phoenix, rising up from flames.
Upon the reverse, these words:

> *Dolor*
> *Nunc*
> *Cinis*

❧ For Improved Health

Upon one face, the rayed Sun
enclosing a circlet of green
leaves. Upon the reverse, these
words:

> *Sic esse*
> *Salubris*

❧ To be Safe from All Harm

Upon one face, an eye rayed with
flames, as the Sun, containing
in its iris a six-pointed star.
Upon the reverse, these words:

> *Dei omnes*
> *Me servant*

❧ To Defy Death by the Power of Life

Upon one face, the rayed Sun
enclosing a death's head. Upon
the reverse, these words:

> *Cras*
> *Mors*
> *Hodie*
> *Sol*

❧ For Wisdom

Upon one face, a serpent curled
head to tail, his circle rayed
with flames. Upon the reverse,
these words:

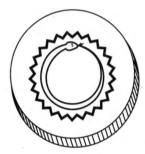

> *Serpens*
> *Sapiens*
> *Scio*
> *Omne*

❧ To Invoke the Sacred Scarab

Upon one face, the Sun rayed
with flames, enclosing a beetle,
as the scarab. Upon the reverse,
these words:

> *Scarabaeus*
> *Soliferus*
> *Salve salve*

🌿 To Celebrate the Season of Spring, as a Source of Fertility

Upon one face, a fountain of water throwing forth leaves. Upon the reverse, these words:

> *Ver fons vitae*
> *Nunc floreo*

🌿 To Win Power

Upon one face, the Sun at the center of a spider's web. Upon the reverse, these words:

> *Omne*
> *Mihi*
> *Venit*

🌿 Against Evil Powers

Upon one face, a Crescent Moon at the center of a spider's web. Upon the reverse, these words:

> *Potentiae*
> *Malae*
> *Vos*
> *Teneo*

❧ To Assume the Powers of the Black Sun

Upon one face, the Sun rayed with black flames. Upon the reverse, these words:

> *Sol obscurus*
> *Mihi*
> *Potentiae tuae*

❧ For Eternal Life

Upon one face, a thrice-branched and thrice-rooted tree, its trunk bearing the symbol of Infinity (thus ∞) while from its three branches rise three flames. Upon the reverse, these words:

> *Ignis vitae*
> *Flagra*
> *In aeternum*

❧ To Be Freed from Habit

Upon one face, the Sun containing a crescent Moon and three stars. Upon the reverse, these words:

> *Ego ipse*
> *Sum*
> *Expletus*

❧ To Vanquish Death

Upon one face, a death's head having a serpent wound through the eye sockets. Upon the reverse, these words:

> *Mors*
> *Te*
> *Mordeo*

❧ To Invoke the Powers of Sun and Moon

Upon one face, the crescent Moon, extended to form a circle, and this circle rayed doubly with flames and swordlike points. Upon the reverse, these words:

> *Aurum soliferum*
> *Argentum luniferum*
> *Nunc huc ades!*

❧ To Celebrate Life

Upon one face, the rayed Sun en-closing an eye rayed with flames. Upon the reverse, these words:

> *Sol omnipotens*
> *Tecum lucesco*

Nine Inscriptions for Amulets Honoring 🌾 *and Invoking the Powers of the Nine Stars* (Stellae Novem)

❧ I, Sirius, the Almighty

Upon one face, a four-rayed star, colored with four colors about a white center—red, green, blue, and yellow. At its center, the fourth character of the runic alphabet (thus, ᚠ). Upon the reverse, these words:

> *Sirius omnipotens*
> *Verum flugens*

❧ II, Mira, the Wondrous

Upon one face, a four-rayed star of orange color. At its center, the twenty-fourth character of the runic alphabet (thus, ᛉ). Upon the reverse, these words:

> *Mira mirabilis*
> *Cratrix miraculorum*

❧ III, Algol, the Demonic

Upon one face, a star having four rays of black color, and a white center, within which, the thirteenth character of the runic alphabet (thus, ⌐). Upon the reverse, these words:

> *Algol anceps*
> *Daemon et dominus*

❧ IV, Spica, the Spiritual

Upon one face, a four-rayed star of blue color; at its center, the sixth character of the runic alphabet (thus, ‹). Upon the reverse, these words:

> *Spica animi*
> *Custos spiriti*

❧ V, Antares, the Fleshly

Upon one face, a four-rayed star of red color. At its center, the third character of the runic alphabet (thus, Þ). Upon the reverse, these words:

> *Antares gigas*
> *Ignis corporis*

🌿 VI, Vega, the Destructive

Upon one face, a four-rayed star of white color. At its center, the tenth character of the runic alphabet (thus, ⟨). Upon the reverse, these words:

> *Vega vidua*
> *Fatum pulchrum*

🌿 VII, Albireo, the Creative

Upon one face, a four-rayed star of green color. At its center, the seventh character of the runic alphabet (thus, ✕). Upon the reverse, these words:

> *Albireo ferax*
> *Vis vitae*

🌿 VIII, Capella, the Wise

Upon one face, a four-rayed star of yellow color. At its center, the eighth character of the runic alphabet (thus, ⟩). Upon the reverse, these words:

> *Capella sapiens*
> *Visus auriferus*

❧ IX, Regulus, the Strong

Upon one face, a four-rayed star
of violet color. At its center, the
twentieth character of the runic
alphabet (thus, ᛗ). Upon the
reverse, these words:

> *Regulus rugitus*
> *Leo caelestis*

Concerning the powers of the Stellae Novem, it may be said
that any earthly desire known to humanity must lie beneath
the influence of some one of these stars. If the proper one be
invoked and honored when it burns in the midnight sky, its
fiery being shall radiate all manner of favors upon one who
beholds it and wears its name upon the breast.

Two Inscriptions for Amulets ❧
to Be Worn on a Thong at the Ankle

❧ To Walk in Harmony with Earth

Upon one face, the Earth sign
(thus, ⊕) within a heart.
Upon the reverse, these words:

> *Cor terrae*
> *Cor meum*

❧ To Walk in the Ways of Truth

Upon one face, an eye rayed as
the Sun. Upon the reverse,
these words:

> *Sic ambulo*
> *In vias*
> *Veritatis*

Twelve Inscriptions Empowered 🌿
by the Ancient Tongue of Tongues

❧ For Riches

Upon one face, the sign of infinity
(thus, ∞) within a four-
sided diamond. Upon the
reverse, these words:

> *Zagin*
> *Zagul*
> *Zagdu*

❧ For Fertility

Upon one face, the Sun
contained within the Moon.
Upon the reverse, these words.

> *Argala*
> *Silmud*
> *Ussa*
> *Argargara*

❧ Against the Sorrows of Mortality

Upon one face, the Sun containing a triangle, which in turn contains an eye. Upon the reverse, these words:

> Arali
> Ilubalagdi
> Pirig
> Pirig

❧ For Wisdom

Upon one face, an eye within the disk of the Sun, whose rays consist of five leaves alternating with five triangles. Upon the reverse, these words:

> Sila pirig
> Namtar agrig

❧ Against Evil

Upon one face, a double axe, from each of whose blades depends a serpent. Upon the reverse, these words:

> Zabin
> Nezaza
> Sentabba

✣ To Inspire Passion

Upon one face, a triangle of three equal sides, two of which point downward. Within its center, a spiral, and growing from its upper side, three flames. Upon the reverse, these words:

> *Ubur inna*
> *Absin galla*
> *Balag ussa*
> *Imrihamun*

✣ For Safety in Travel

Upon one face, a double triangle, set vertically point to point, and behind it curled waters of the sea. Upon the reverse, these words:

> *Zuab*
> *Garin*
> *Sila*

🦎 For Power

Upon one face, a circle containing at its center a double triangle, as above, each containing
an eye, with Crescent Moons
set flanking this figure. Upon the
reverse, these words:

> *Astar*
> *Zagdu*
> *Arauna*

🦎 To Summon the Dead

Upon one face, a half-circle set
horizontally, from which rises
a triangle, upon which lies
the crescent Moon on its back
throwing forth three flames.
Upon the reverse, these words:

> *Arali*
> *Sila*
> *Ziga*

✣ For Protection from Fire and Water

Upon one face, a circle from which emanate curled waters of the sea, and within this, the Sun containing the Earth sign. Upon the reverse, these words:

> *Umu zuab*
> *Adda pirig*
> *Ag ag ag*

✣ To Soften a Hard Heart

Upon one face, a circle with curled waters, as above, containing two triangles pointing one above and one below, between which are set three orbs as of Sun, Moon, and Earth. Upon the reverse, these words:

> *Astar*
> *Zagdu*
> *Zuab*

🐏 To Invoke the Powers of the Goat

Upon one face, a triangle pointing downward, containing an eye and crowned on its upper side with two curved flames. Also edged on its other two sides with flames, and this whole figure set upon the point of a smaller triangle pointing upward. Upon the reverse, these words:

> *Azag*
> *Dara*
> *Sanga*

Thrice a Dozen Charms

As HAS BEEN suggested within this book before, a charm finds strength not only in its component materials but also in the manner of its fashioning. Therefore do not hasten carelessly to perform what should be slowly and meticulously wrought. The charm will gain power, as does a seed, most fruitfully where all is well prepared for its unfolding and its flowering. Heed, then, the circumstances, the words of invocation, and the means to best employment of all procedures that shall be here described.

A Charm to Invoke the Powers of the Earth

After rain, when the Earth has received enough water to be soft, thus clinging to the fingers and to itself, go out and gather up enough to fill the bowl of a large spoon. Bring this into the house, and quickly mold it into a sphere, smooth and rounded evenly. Set it aside in an iron vessel, this covered over with a square of rough sackcloth, and when it has dried, after a day or two, remove it and place it in the center of the cloth, with these as well: a small green twig broken thrice, a soft white feather of down, and a drop of blood pricked from your own finger. Over them, then, speak words to work the enchantment:

> *Now earth is earth*
> *And earth is air*
> *And earth is water*
> *And earth is fire:*
> *Let all go into thee*
> *And all be thine*
> *Let all arise from thee*
> *And then be mine.*

Now fold the cloth to enclose these four entities, and bind it up with a lashing of coarse twine. This charm should be kept in a dark drawer or box, to be taken out and in cupped hands held to the breast, and its words repeated, whenever a strengthening influence is to be called forth.

A Charm to Win the Moon's Aid 🌿 for a Secret Purpose

A small globe of crystal or clear uncolored glass must first be consecrated by holding it up to the light of the Full Moon, that the lunar image may be caught therein. After this has been performed, the sphere shall serve for a charm to pro-

cure the secret wishes of its owner. Thus, on the night of
each New Moon, hold the sphere in the left palm, by candlelight, gaze upon it, and say this:

> *Crescent be full*
> *And crystal fill:*
> *Thus my eye*
> *And thus my will:*
> *Fiat voluntas abdita*
> *Fiat voluntas abdita*
> *Fiat voluntas abdita*

The sphere should then be kept in a small bag of leather
inscribed with figures of the Moon's phases, and worn tied
to a thong about the neck during those days and nights
between the crescent and the full. While it is not being
worn, this charm should be kept wrapped in a black cloth
and hidden away.

A Charm to Win Immortality from the Sun 🌿

Find a beetle that takes its shape from the ancient scarab. It
were best if it should have a metallic luster
and hue, as of the Japanese beetle
that feeds upon the rose. Put it to
death by drowning some hours in a
tincture of musk and alcohol. Remove it
then, and arrange it carefully upon a
small cloth of red silk, set in a sunny place,

to dry there for three days. After this, the beetle upon the silk should be laid before three gold candles, lighted at midnight, and these words said:

> *Scarab of sun*
> *Dark death is done*
> *Gold life begun*

Wrap the beetle in the silk, along with a spoonful, each, of these: pollen from the sunflower, rose petals, orris root, salt, and myrrh. Then tie the packet up with a golden thread or ribbon. It should be placed within a small wooden box, which is then sealed with melted beeswax and an image of the Sun inscribed upon its lid. If this charm be kept beneath the pillow for seven days, it shall renew the spirit of anyone who rests the head there. Henceforth, the box should be safely kept and each year consecrated anew, with the same words, before three gold candles at midnight upon the Summer Solstice.

A Charm to Drive Away Evil 🌿

Take an iron nail, red-rusted by time and rain, and forged by hand in the ancient form (if such can be found); on a dark night, moonless and cloudy, set down this nail upon a smallish flat stone, and with an iron hammer strike it thrice, at each stroke saying this:

> *Clavus ferreus*
> *Malleus ferreus*

Ferrum rufulum
Ferrum nobilis

Score the stone thrice across with the nail's point, then take the stone away quickly and bury it in the Earth far from your house. The nail should afterwards be carried with you always, as a charm against evil influences and emanations.

A Charm to Form an Alliance with the Trees 🌾

When summer falters before its flight, go on an evening of full moonlight, and cut from an oak tree one true branch, thick with leaves and with acorns bunched. Then where a wood grows dense and dark, stand at its edge and the oak bough shake—saying these words to the ranks of trees, that their strength may be yours for whatever you please:

With oak I lead
That ash may follow
Also alder
Elm and willow
Cedar and locust
Hickory, larch,
Walnut, chestnut
Poplar, birch,
Beech and maple
Fir and pine:
All these powers
So be mine.

Then hang the oak bough over your door, taking one acorn from its store to be sewn up fast in a chamois skin, safe to be kept for what you would win.

A Charm to Rid the Mind ❦ or the Body of an Affliction

Gather a quart of water from some spring or stream, and pour it into a large bowl, set within a darkened chamber; by candlelight, then, take a silver knife and write with its point upon the water's surface the name of that which afflicts you. Next, soak a small lock of lamb's wool first in a sweet-scented oil and second in some red wine. Carry it to the bowl and drop it into the water, saying these words:

> *The dark be lightened*
> *The harsh be softened*
> *The rank be sweetened*
> *By the power of the knife*
> *And by the power of the water.*

Leave the lamb's wool there to soak all night, until sunrise, when it should be removed, wrung out, and set to dry upon a small circle of white velvet cloth. Meanwhile, the contents of the bowl should be emptied out into a hole dug in the Earth, and the hole filled in again. When the lamb's wool is quite dry it should be sewn up in the velvet and pinned beneath your clothing, to be worn there for a full month, and thereafter kept elsewhere in safety, that its charmed powers may not be diminished through neglect.

A Charm to Bind an Enemy 🌾

Gather from the corners of your chambers every cobweb, and place them, all of a tangle, upon a black cloth. Procure then a fly, recently dead, and set it down upon the mass of webs. These words should then be written down on paper:

> *North south east west*
> *Spider's web shall bind him best*
> *East west north south*
> *Hold his limbs and stop his mouth*
> *Seal his eyes and choke his breath*
> *Wrap him round with ropes of death.*

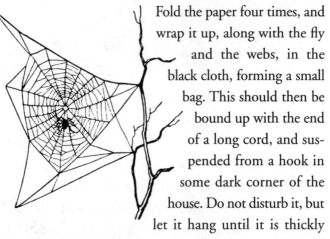

Fold the paper four times, and wrap it up, along with the fly and the webs, in the black cloth, forming a small bag. This should then be bound up with the end of a long cord, and suspended from a hook in some dark corner of the house. Do not disturb it, but let it hang until it is thickly covered with dust. Then it may be taken down and buried in the Earth, to work its influence in perpetual secrecy.

A Charm for Fertility 🌿

In early spring, twigs of the alder, bedecked with new red catkins, should be gathered in the first light of morning. Place them in a vessel of water, and set this upon a good-sized mirror near a window where the Sun may fall. Each morning thereafter collect with a feather the grains of golden pollen that have been spilt upon the mirror, and save these gleanings carefully within a folded paper. When no more pollen appears, take what has been gathered and put it into a small bag of yellow silk, along with the same paper, on which these words should be written:

> *Pollicitum pollinis*
> *Pollentia pollinis*
> *Pollentia appollinis*
> *Pollis appollinis*
> *Pollinem polluceo*
> *Polleo polleo*

Hang up this bag above your bed, and keep it there until a child shall be conceived; then the charm must be burned in a small fire of alderwood, and its ashes strewn over that spot where the catkins were gathered.

A Charm to Transform Death into Life 🌿

When it is dark on a summer's night, gather three long strands of ivy where they trail upon stones or trees or the Earth. Bring them into a chamber where one green candle is lighted, and twist the vines into a wreath to fit upon the head. Next, in a mortar crush some white chalk to a powder, and dust the hands and face with a little of this. Then these words should be spoken:

> *White of bone*
> *Dark of shade*
> *Of dust and night*
> *My death is made*
> *Death my self*
> *Death my peer*

IVY

What I hold
I do not fear
So bone to flesh
And shade to leaf
Death my dear
I give thee life.

Carefully unbind the strands of ivy, and set their cut ends in a jug of water, leaving them so for two weeks; meanwhile save the crushed chalk that remains. When the time has passed, plant the three ivies at the foot of a large oak tree, and when this is done sprinkle the chalk about them with these words:

Bone be flesh
Shade be leaf
As death is mine
It bears me life.

Water and attend these charmed vines faithfully, and they shall give to your present life a strength as the oak's, and to your ultimate death a fruitfulness denying all night and dust.

A Charm to Procure the Heart's Desire ❧

In wet weather walk over the fields, and where the great white mushrooms rise up flat and wide, gather the greatest

cap and carry it home. That night, by candlelight, take a
large needle and with it scratch this, small, upon the mushroom's upper skin:

> *Flesh of darkness*
> *Born of death*
> *Give my will*
> *Thy life and breath*
> *Wither dry*
> *And shrink to dust*
> *My hearth shall feed*
> *Upon thy crust.*

Breathe upon this inscription, and then lock the mushroom
away safely for the rest of that night. The next morning,
take a sharp knife and chop the whole into many little
pieces. Spread them out in an iron pan and set them in a
warm oven until they are quite dry. Then sew them up in a
bag of red cloth, and each night thereafter wear this charm
over the heart, until the desired effect is accomplished. When
it has been fulfilled, the charm should be taken back and
buried near the spot where the mushroom was gathered.

A Charm for a Renewal of the Spirit 🌼

This shall be done in winter, when leaves are dead and the
spirit dark. Bring home from a willow tree that stands by
frozen water twelve live wands, stand them in a vessel of
water, and feed them with new water every morning until

their leaves are born anew from the dormant buds. While these are soft and of a pale green, strip them all from the twigs and with a pestle, in a mortar, pound them to a paste. Spread this out in a shallow dish, set at a sunny window, and when the paste is dry, powder it in the same mortar where it was first prepared. Add some sweet scented oil, a few drops, to this dust, and then, at night, burn it as an offering before twelve yellow candles. While it burns, say this:

> *All that was dead is not dead.*
> *All that was dark is not dark.*
> *The spirit is a fire. The spirit is eternal.*
> *The spirit is one spirit—the spirit of all spirits,*
> *And that one holds the fire of the cosmos.*
> *Breathe here now, and so shall the cosmos breathe,*
> *And of its own breath shall the cosmos be made anew.*

Save the ashes of the incense in a small wooden box, tied about with threads of gold, and keep it always near as a charm to invoke the influences of the foregoing ceremony all year long.

A Charm for Recalling the Faithless 🌸

At midnight light a new black candle in a locked chamber. Take the white wing feather of a dove or pigeon and dip it in some pungent scented oil, rue, wintergreen, or the like. Then let its tip burn in the candle flame, and say these words:

Thy flight be stayed
Thy wing be bound
This cloud casts thee
To the ground.

Dip the feather again into the oil, then break it into small pieces and fold these up in a bit of silver paper. Bind this charm with black thread, and bury it in the ground near your doorstep. So shall it call the faithless one back, and when returned, drops of the same oil must be touched to the brow and the palms of that person, who then shall not leave again. Yet reveal not the reason for this anointment, lest its power be diminished.

A Charm to Nourish the Wits 🦋
and Renew the Powers

You must go in late summer to certain rank stream beds or low pasturelands to seek out the blue vervain, whose flowers are small and near purple and whose stem is four-sided. Pluck this herb, several stalks of it, and bring these into the chamber where your works are most often performed. Here four candles of violet hue shall be lighted, and an oil of sweet lavender, in a dish, set in readiness. Bare the floor of this chamber, and inscribe upon it in blue chalk a large circle. In its center set the oil and the stalks of vervain, also a good length of black cord. Then step into the circle, and with the chalk write these words small around its inner circumference:

Verbena hastata
Quattuor elementa
Quattuor loci
Hasta verbena
Viam monstra

Next bind up the stalks of vervain with the cord spiralled
about their full length, to make
a thick wand. Dip its flowered
end into the oil and with it
retrace the circle, anointing its
boundary well with sweetness.

VERVAIN   The circle, so charmed, should
then be covered up and hidden by a rug or carpet, to be
preserved until time shall wear it away, and the wand of
vervain hung up over the entrance to this chamber, that it
may direct the ways of the one who passes and repasses
beneath it. So shall the influence of this ancient herb be
fixed there, and the wisdom it conjures arise perpetually in
those surroundings.

A Charm to Work Revenge ❧

Gather from the hawthorn tree, or from some great thorned
rose, three thorns of noble length. Set them to steep in an
oil of civet, and meanwhile take the heart from a fowl which
has been readied for the cooking pot and seethe it in white

vinegar over the fire. When the heart is well boiled, remove it, and put it into the oil with the thorns, to remain there until the last stroke of midnight, at which moment light three black candles, and soon plunge the three thorns into the heart, with each thrust saying one of these:

> *This shames the deed*
> *This blames the hand*
> *This blights the heart.*

Wrap the pierced heart in a scrap of ragged cloth, and dig for it a grave in some waste place where weeds flourish and rubbish lies strewn about. This charm so buried is most deadly, and shall bring such ruin to its victim that it should not be undertaken without serious consideration of the consequences. The effect may be lessened, and a weaker form of revenge worked upon its object, if the heart, once pierced, be not interred but rather preserved in a small vial of the oil in which it was steeped. Some single misfortune then, and not such dire devastation, shall befall the one in whose name the charm is kept.

A Charm to Win Another's Love 🌿

Take of violet blossoms, shorn from their stems, a great handful, and spread them upon a red paper to dry for a fortnight, or longer if need be. When they are quite curled and crisp, grind them in a mortar to dust, and mix this well with two dozen blanched almonds pounded to a paste, and a little clear honey to bind all together. Then from this confection shall several small cakes be shaped. Wrap up each cake closely in silver paper; tie it about with a purple thread, and pack all these sweets into a small box, itself then to be wrapped in silver and tied with purple. When these preparations are completed, set the box upon the same sheet of red paper, on which now a circle has been drawn and these words inscribed in its center:

> *Viola violae*
> *Tinctus animae*
> *Custos laetitiae*
> *Leno amoris*

Turn the box thrice about, raise it thrice in the air, thrice repeat aloud the words written on the paper, and finally kiss the box nine times. Then it may be sent (but secretly, for the identity of its giver should remain hidden) to the one whose love is sought. The inscribed paper should be folded small and kept beneath your pillow, until its purpose is well accomplished.

A Charm to Win Honor and 🌿 Favor in the Eyes of Others

Fill an iron pot with fine, dry sand taken from a bank or pit, but not from the sea, and set it down in bright sunlight. Then with a lodestone or magnet stir the sand about, and if it be an Earth of high virtue certain grains of iron will cling to the lodestone when it is drawn forth. Remove them into a white bowl, and stir the sand again to draw further particles of iron from it. Continue the gleaning until a small spoonful of this substance has been obtained. Then empty it out upon the center of a circular piece of red silk, and over it set a small paper bearing these words written in red ink:

> *Metal of strength*
> *Blood of earth*
> *Out of death*
> *I draw thee forth:*
> *I honor thee*
> *Now favor me.*

Tie up the paper, folded, and the iron dust, within the red silk, and wear this charm on a red cord about your neck for twenty-eight days and twenty-eight nights. Then untie it, and pour out the iron into a shallow dish of water. After three days collect the rust that has formed, and with it stain the palms of your hands. This influence will not soon pass away, and should attract warm regard from all whom you encounter.

A Charm to Cure the Body of Sundry Ailments ❧

Take a lump of beeswax as big as your thumb, warm it until it is softened, and fashion it into a human figure. Before a lighted white candle, when the night is dark, hold this figure in the left hand and anoint it with a tincture of aloes.

Then dip it into a small bowl of honey, sprinkle it with ground white pepper and with powdered turmeric, and quickly wind it about entirely with a ribbon of white silk, after which it should be wrapped tightly in a small piece of white cloth. Leave it thus before the burning candle for a full hour. During this time, prepare a bath of hot water, and in it dissolve a teaspoonful each of the aloes, the honey, the pepper, and the turmeric. Lie down in this water quietly until it begins to grow cool; then arise, dry yourself, and dress in clothing that is entirely of white. Return to the burning candle, and say these words before it:

> *The bitter cures*
> *The sweet cures*
> *The silver cures*
> *The gold cures*
> *The dark cures*
> *The light cures*
> *The warm cures*
> *The white cures*
> *Thus am I renewed this night*
> *And through all others soon*
> *And late.*

Blow out the candle, and take the wax figure in its wrappings to your bed, where it should be kept beneath the pillow from that night until two Full Moons have risen. Thus it may serve to charm certain ills from the body, while more baths of the same nature should be taken often for their excellent salubrity.

A Charm to Win Control Over Another 🌾

Paint with a brush and India ink, upon a ragged scrap of cloth, the figure of the person you would control. Furl the cloth into a scroll, tie it with a thread of black, and curl this up into a tightly rolled coil. Wrap the coil in a vine leaf, and this in a scrap of red silk, and this in a circle cut from silver foil. Wind it round with red thread, seal it well with sealing wax, and pack it in a hollow walnut shell. Set both halves together tight with glue and then with wax again, and mark this on the nut to fix the spell:

> *Nux nox*
> *Pax pox*
> *Hex hax*
> *Wix wax*
> *Hithero hothero*
> *Withero wothero*
> *Well.*

Shut the nut within a box, bound about by heavy twine, and you shall hold the subject in your rule. So shall he do as you command, a feckless shadow to your hand, though he be fabled king or common fool.

A Charm to Keep a Cat from Straying ❦

To win the faith and affection of a cat, her dignity and over-weening wit notwithstanding, you must please her and make her smile. Your way of charming must amuse and entertain her while it takes her fancy and so claims her. Therefore, dry for some days in a clean white bowl thirteen leaves of good unblemished catnip—none that has been broken, or trodden, or neglected among weeds, but for preference that which you have planted in a decent corner of the garden—for her pleasure. When the leaves are dry, crush them to powder with a silver spoon, and mix them into a spoonful of fat from some fine hen or duck or goose, or else into an ounce of best butter. When this ointment is stirred smooth, let it rest for an hour or so. Meanwhile, invite the cat to sit upon a table in your kitchen. Set before her a small dish of cream, a few ounces of cooked fish, and a morsel of raw beef, and while she eats them say this to her:

> *Grimalkin grimalkin*
> *Feasted in my kitchen*
> *There shalt thou stay*
> *Nor from it care to stray.*

When she has finished, stroke her back thrice and collect the hairs of fur that cling to your hand. Fold them up in a paper, and put them in a safe place. Then, kneeling on the floor and holding the cat, anoint her paws with the mixture of fat and catnip. Carry her to your door and set her free then; she shall soon wash her paws with relish and laughter, and her good humor thereafter compliments your deed. Next take the paper in which her fur is folded, and write upon it those same words which were said over her feasting. Seal it up with wax and a seal, and keep it hidden somewhere so she may not find it, thus to bind her in secrecy as well as openly by her consent.

A Charm to Gain Wealth 🌿

When a fresh hen has been dressed for the stew pot, save one of its feet and while it is still of a fresh yellow, rub it well with whiskey and with salt. Place within its claws a new silver coin, and also a scrap of paper on which this is written:

> *Hen hen*
> *Give me gain*

> *Thus to hold*
> *Silver and gold.*

Curl up the claws and tie them about with black cord so that all they contain is secure. Then hang this charm by the same cord from some eave of your house, and it shall draw money there within the year.

A Charm to Warm the Affections of Another ❧

When snow falls swift and dry, a cloth of red velvet should be cut into the shape of a heart, as wide as your hand. Go out and stand in a place where the flakes may float down freely, then hold out the heart upon your palm, saying this:

> *Star, crystal*
> *Silver stone*
> *I warm thee now*
> *To blood and rain*
> *Nor shalt thou turn*
> *To ice again.*

Return into the house, there breathing upon the snowflakes that cover the velvet until they have melted into drops of water; then fold up the cloth into a triangle and pin it with a golden pin, so to remain while every day thereafter the same words shall be spoken over it anew. When its purpose is accomplished, the next charm should soon be worked to strengthen and preserve its influence, as shall be shown.

A Charm to Bind the Affections of Another 🌿

Pluck from the roadside or some neglected plot of ground an old and withered stalk of burdock burrs. Pick off three round burrs, lightly, with cautious fingers, and set them down, each separated from the other, on a table of bare wood. There light three red candles, and carry to them the charm of velvet cloth earlier prepared. Unpin it and unfold it; then spread it flat beside the burrs, and set the three upon the velvet's center, one by one, while these three verses are said:

> *This thine eye*
> *I bind to me*
>
> *This thy hand*
> *I bind to me*
>
> *This thy heart*
> *I bind to me*
> *Ever and ever and forever.*

BURDOCK

Move the burrs to lie together, fixed and locked to one another, and likewise all three to the center of the cloth. Then fold up the cloth about them and pin it tight. This charm should then be locked away in a drawer or cupboard, and not disturbed again for fear of loosening its bonds about the one so enchanted.

A Charm to Cause a Proposal of Marriage 🌿

To work this charm you should gather twelve red cherries from a tree, or if the cherries must be bought they should soon be washed clean, first in white wine and then in water. Set them in a green bowl, and give them to be eaten by the one whom you would marry. Eat none yourself, but be sure the subject eats them all, and let the cherry stones be saved within the bowl. After he or she has gone away, take the twelve stones and wash them clean; then set them in the Sun to blanch. When they are white and fair, spread them out at night upon a

CHERRIES

small cloth of red velvet, before twelve red candles. With a fine quill and black ink, mark these words upon them, one letter to each stone:

Sponsalia mea

A few drops of sweet scented oil, best of all from flowers of the tuberose, should be sprinkled over the cloth, and then the stones enclosed within it, and the bag thus formed, bound at the neck with red thread. This charm should then be tied onto a gold chain and worn, concealed, as a necklace until a proposal of marriage is called forth. After which it may be undone, and the cherry stones planted in the Earth to ensure that this betrothal be perpetually fruitful.

A Charm to Be Given as a Pledge of Love 🌿

Procure twelve branches, full berried, from the holly tree, and set them in water between two gold candles, which should be lighted early in the evening and allowed to burn down to their sockets. When they are consumed, pluck all the berries from the branches into a goblet. Then thread a fine needle with a red thread, whose single length shall be twice twenty-four inches, drawing it through the eye until it is double and knotting the ends together. With this needle quickly prick the tip of the fourth finger of your left hand until a drop of blood can be squeezed forth. Anoint the thread with this blood, saying:

> *Fruit of ruby*
> *Pearl of blood*
> *Red of love*
> *Thy gift I give*

Then string the berries onto the thread, taking care not to break them open, and when all are evenly strung together cut free the needle and tie the ends of the thread in a sturdy triple knot. Then this necklace should be hung up near the fire to dry and grow firm. As soon as it is so cured, it should be packed up in a small wooden box with those words said earlier inscribed upon the lid. So should it be given as a pledge of love to another, but with care, for ill shall befall anyone who gives this token and betrays it before a year has passed.

A Charm to Turn Aside Evil and Ill Fortune 🌿

The mountain ash or rowan tree has long been honored for its power against evil forces. It should ever be treated with respect, that its favor be not turned against the one who employs its strength. In late summer, when the tree is heavy with red fruit (the yellow variety is of a weaker influence), seek out one branch that leans toward the south, and shake it gently until it shall let fall four berries. Gather these up, and also take four of the leaves, carry all indoors, and soon build a fire of good birch or apple wood upon your hearth. When the blaze is ripe and golden, cast one of the rowan berries into the flames, along with one of the leaves, saying this:

> *Virtue is mine, as of this tree*
> *Beware the fire I cast at thee*

Cast in the second berry, and a leaf, saying:

> *Wisdom is mine, as of this tree*
> *Beware the fire I cast at thee*

Cast in the third, both berry and leaf, saying:

> *Power is mine, as of this tree*
> *Beware the fire I cast at thee*

Take then the fourth leaf and fruit, and roast them slowly in an iron pot over the fire until they are dried and blackened. Cool them, and wrap their remains in a red cloth, which charm should soon be buried in the Earth near your threshold. Thus it shall protect the house and those who dwell therein from whatever evil emanations might dare to stray too near.

A Charm to Turn Back the Spirits of the Dead 🦋

Where the mistletoe cleaves to some living tree, there to feed its many berries, fleshed pale and waxen as the flesh of corpses, you must go in company (for to go alone would be perilous) and wrench from their fastenings a few stems well furnished with white fruit. Carry them home, and spread them out at night up on a table covered with a black cloth. Set at random in their midst five black candles, burning, and at their center a clear glass vessel. Bring then to the table all of these: a red wine of the Medoc, a strained tincture of red carnation petals infused in alcohol, an oil of red storax, and five fragments of bone. Set them down in a row, and speak this incantation:

> *Flesh lacking blood*
> *Bone lacking flesh*
> *Spirit lacking bone*
> *Arise and be fed*
> *Arise to bone and flesh and blood*
> *This night renewed by mortal food*
> *Nevermore to thirst for mine*
> *Nor on my living limbs to twine*

Mix in the central vessel the wine, tincture, oil, and bone, and sprinkle a little of this potion over all the sprigs of mistletoe. Then, before cockcrow, bear the vessel, and the sprigs wrapped closely in the black tablecloth, away to a burial ground, where, between two graves, the mistletoe should be laid down gently, unwrapped, and the vessel's contents emptied over it. Pluck five of the mistletoe's berries then, to carry home; but leave all else among the dead, there to find fit surroundings instead of where you dwell. The five berries should be preserved in a small vial of red storax oil, and kept always near at hand to calm and turn back any rash spirit who should presume to visit you thereafter.

A Charm for Eternal Youth 🌿

Go to a grove of pines, when the Moon is new, and in the Earth beneath their boughs inscribe a circle, wide as you are tall. Lie down within it, your arms extended to meet the circle's rim, and say these words:

> *The ancient pine*
> *Is evergreen*
> *The crescent moon*
> *May never wane*
> *The circle bound*
> *Is ever round*
> *And so my life*
> *As light and leaf*

Pluck three needles of pine from a green branch, take them home, and wind them tightly round about with a hair from

your head and a long green thread. Keep this charm beside
your bed, that you may dream of eternity, and each night
before you sleep, repeat the words that have conjured youth
from the enchanted grove. Ever after, you should wear some
token of green—jade, emerald, or other stone, ornament, or
article of clothing—in honor of this fair spell now threaded
through your life.

A Charm to Reveal Truth 🌿 among False Appearances

When a young fowl has been roasted and eaten, take the
carcass all its bones, and boil these for six hours until the
flesh shall slip away. Further scrub the bones clean, freeing
each rib and joint from its fastenings, and then let all lie on
a paper in the Sun until they are quite dry and white. When
these bones are so prepared, place them in a box of black
wood and set it down before a single white candle. Gaze
into the flame, while considering earnestly all manifesta-
tions of that situation from which you would draw the
truth. When all these various aspects have arisen before your
eyes, take from the box a bone, and inscribe upon it in India
ink one possible truth. Next take others, and write upon
them the other truths you have envisioned. Then before the
candle set out all the bones in a row, and say this over them:

> *Beneath the flesh of confusion,*
> *Behold the bones of that which is true:*
> *Still all save one are false,*

And must deceive where the spirit's eye is shut:
Yet open now that eye
And the true bone shall rise revealed

Replace the inscribed bones in the box, and also all others that remain unmarked, and shake the box to mix them well. Then with the eyes shut, draw from within one bone, on which shall be written the single truth. If it should bear no inscription, all of the supposed truths are false, and the situation must be studied in a new light after a fortnight has passed. Whatever bone was drawn forth, it should this day be hung from a cord in some window where the Sun will cast its shadow upon an opposite wall. Let it remain there, serving to charm the brain and eye to clear vision thereafter, in all instances of concealment or confusion.

A Charm to Break Some Troublesome Habit 🌾

You must take a white egg, and, through small holes made in each end, blow forth the contents from the shell. Plug up one hole with a little softened beeswax, then fill the shell, using a fine funnel, with sour red wine. Carefully seal the second hole with more wax, and in red ink write upon the surface of the shell the name of that plaguing compulsion you would be rid of. Take this egg in secret then to a place where great rocks cover the ground. Stand there and say these words:

Halls of blood where life has fled
Walls of bone that close me round
I break thy reign, thy yoke I shed
I cast thy powers to the ground

Hurl the egg against a rock so that it shall burst into fragments and the contents be spilt upon the Earth. Then gather up the broken bits of shell, take them home, and grind them to a powder in a mortar. This charmed dust should be kept within a small jar, a pinch of it to be placed upon the tongue and swallowed whenever further treacherous temptations may appear.

A Charm to Assuage Anger and Ill-Feeling 🌿

A smooth stone, smaller than your fist, should be sought out in the bed of a clear stream or dug up from the garden's soil. Soak it in a solution of salt and water, scrub it well, dry it in the Sun, and then inscribe upon it these words, in green ink:

Now anger melt
In tears of salt
Be turned to love
By this sweet salve

Lave the stone on every side with the cool sap crushed from seven leaves of stonecrop, until even the inscription has been washed away, and then further anoint it with an oil of verbena. It may then be wrapped in green silk and secreted in some drawer or cupboard used by the one whose anger you would assuage; or, if the anger afflicts you yourself, sleep with the charm beneath your pillow for seven nights, after which time it should be kept concealed in your own drawer or cupboard.

A Charm to Waste Another's Wealth 🌱

When the mandrake, known also as May apple, unfolds its leaves over the dark floor of the wood, yet before it flowers or bears fruit, dig up one plant,

leaves and stem and root, this last with poisoned humors laden, keeping about it the clod of wet earth to which it clings. Take all home in a stout bag, and there remove the root, saving the soil, but breaking and casting away both

MAY APPLE

stem and leaves. Wash clean the root's deadly flesh, and let it for a week lie still to wilt somewhat. Then mark upon it, in black ink, the name of the one whose wealth you would destroy (yet let this deed be done for reasons other than mere petty envy, lest your own possessions wilt and fall away as well). Then take the earth you have preserved, and in a bowl, with a little water, mix it to thick mud; therein plunge the root, covering it over well. Remove it, let this plaster dry, then plunge it in to be again well coated; and still a third time work this plastering, so that the root shall be encased within a triple shroud. Wrap it then in ragged cloths, and keep this charm in darkness until the season when the May apple bears its fruit in that same wood. Go then and pluck one of these little apples, bring it home, and in the presence of the mummied root, taste of the fruit in triumph, scornfully, with laughter, saying:

> *So must he waste and mourn his loss*
> *While I may flourish in his sight*
> *A gall to his afflicted flesh*
> *His darkness mocked before my light*

A Charm to Dispel a State of Melancholy 🌿

Fill a large earthenware pot with soft dark loam, and over its surface sprinkle seeds of grass, gathered from the fields or bought, if need be, but all of them fat and fertile. Set the pot in a sunny window, and water it each day at dawn, saying these words:

> *Out of night*
> *Shines the grass*
> *So my darkness*
> *Now may pass*
> *And change to joy*
> *That drinks the sun*
> *As gold that from*
> *His side doth run*

When the grass has risen high and put forth good foliage, clip half its number and make of this an infusion within a small teapot, letting the leaves steep in the water for full fifteen minutes. Sweeten this tea with honey, and drink it slowly, meditating on the Sun that has given life to all leaves, and that same Sun toward which your spirit turns anew. The next morning clip the remaining leaves and hang them to dry in a dim corner. Afterwards preserve them in a small canister, that they may sustain your joy through the days to come, never permitting their solar influence to depart again.

A Charm to Possess Potency and Passion 🌿

The dried skin sloughed from the body of a serpent should be procured by two who are betrothed, or if they seek this in vain, a strip of silver cloth may be used instead. Flatten it out upon a table, and cover it thickly with these: dried grass blades, leaves of tea, leaves of sage, seeds of anise, and a few flakes of hot red pepper. The skin should then be rolled up lengthwise to enclose its contents, and sewed tight with a thread of purple. The long serpent so created shall next be taken and hidden beneath the mattress of the bridal bed, while the lovers recite these words:

> *O serpent wise*
> *Thy flesh doth rise*
> *To warm the bed*
> *Where we shall wed*

Then upon the nuptial night, the two shall bring forth this serpent into candlelight and make an anointment of his body with sweet tinctures of musk and ambergris. Then they shall hold him up over a wide bowl or basin, and pull out the thread that binds him together, letting the herbs within fall down into the bowl. These should then be infused in boiling wine to brew a potion, which shall presently be strained, clear and drunk slowly. Finally, the two, in nakedness, shall anoint each other entirely with the same tinctures, after which the marriage may be consummated. Thus shall the serpent at last be led to redeem that flesh of mankind which from antiquity, by sustained venoms, he has so slyly betrayed.

A Charm to Increase Beauty 🌿

When you may happen upon the split shell of the locust or
cicada clinging to a tree, remove it, taking care not to break
it in any part, and preserve it in a box. Then when you have
need of it, set it forth in a large brass bowl before a gold candle burning, and pour over it these scented oils, a few drops
of each: jasmine, tuberose, narcissus, rose, and gardenia.
Touch the locust then with the candle flame, setting it afire,
and say these words:

> *Dead thing, evil, old and dried*
> *This foul skin be cast aside*

And thus transformed to golden fire
New and young and fine and fair

When this fire goes out, take the ashes remaining in the bowl and crush them to a paste among the dregs of oil; then tip the candle to drip wax into the bowl, to a spoonful or so, blending this with the other substances while the mixture cools and thickens. All should then be scraped together and formed with the fingers into a ball, this to be wrapped up in fine silk and kept in a drawer near the mirror where your face is most often reflected. Each time henceforth when you look in this mirror, repeat the words of the incantation, and afterwards dose your eyes for a dozen seconds before looking again. The beneficial effect shall soon be worked if the words are said slowly, and if the scented charm be passed to and fro before the face while they are repeated.

A Charm to Recall the Dead, in the Name of Love

If it be possible, a letter once written by the one who has died should be found, or else an article of clothing, or picture if a good likeness, or some book, worn from his or her touch. Cut from whatever memento is procured a few comers or shreds to make a spoonful of snippets, and bring these at night, with fine incenses of myrrh and sandalwood, to a table where seven white candles are burning. Sprinkle the snippets over the incense, all contained within a vessel of brass, and then set these alight with one of the candle flames. While they burn, speak these words:

The presence in this room
Denies both time and tomb
Thy shade before my eyes
Bright as flame doth rise
Nor shall it cool or pale
Until my life must fail.

When these substances have all ceased to burn, their ashes should be gathered into a box and the candles left to consume themselves entirely. Soon after this you must buy a new gold locket on a chain of gold, and place within it a pinch of ashes from the box, while repeating the words of the previous ritual. Thereafter the locket should never be opened again, but worn always about your neck to be warmed by the warmth of your own life. Thus shall your devotion confer comfort upon the beloved dead wherever he or she may lie, and likewise that presence upon your breast that shall work your own grief's assuagement. Any ashes that are left within the box may be scattered upon the west wind, where they shall meet that departed but immortal spirit flowing ever toward the Sun.

Ceremonies
for the Year

HERE, LASTLY, SHALL follow twelve brief symbolic rites, in which some of the foregoing ideas and practices find expression, expansion, and elevation. The complete cycle, moreover, may be seen ultimately to transcend all of its individual parts—about which more will be said presently.

There are no strict requirements for the settings and circumstances surrounding these rituals, save that they be performed in a chamber providing sufficient seclusion, silence, and space for their best realization. Let such a room be as free as possible from furniture and other distracting elements, and see that there be dark hangings at the windows that can be drawn entirely. All doors to the chamber should be closed and even locked.

That which shall serve as the altar may be merely a stout table, great enough to bear all the objects necessary to the ceremony. As will be seen, a cloth of some description covers this altar on every occasion; therefore the table itself need not be of great beauty. It may, however, be set upon a low platform if one should be available. Thus its importance, and the significance of what it bears, shall appear the greater. The floor before the altar should be cleared, allowing sufficient space for all celebrants to stand well back from the area where the one who leads the ritual shall be passing to and fro.

The proper time for each ceremony is indicated within its description here, and should be adhered to as closely as possible; however, if this exact time is not convenient, it may be adjusted somewhat, so long as the time substituted is appropriate to the requirements of the ritual. It should also be added that if for some reason the actual performance of these rituals is not possible, they may be read through, aloud or silently, upon the proper occasion, thus to be visualized and contemplated. Their benefit shall even so be gained.

There is nothing of pure invention in these ceremonies, nothing that does not in some way grow out of the unchanging truths of the universe, the solar system, the Earth and its yearly cycle of seasons. Through even these brief rituals it may well be seen how the year and its seasons follow a pattern directly related to the life of human beings, as it may also be said that they live their life according to the great cycle of the year and this naturally, for they are no less a part of such seasonal events than is the Earth itself.

Earth's long ritual, performed in twelve phases and set
in the mode of highest tragedy, is our human ritual as well,
and if we follow this course, celebrating in turn each phase
of Earth's great truth, we may then also strengthen knowledge of ourselves and of all our life. For out of these twelve
phases or fractional truths springs the one great truth—
that immutable design of creation, destruction, and rebirth
which time does not alter, which continues year after year
within even the very spirit of human beings, whether they
perceive it or not.

For those who will recognize them, there are comfort
and encouragement, as well as inspiration, to be found
within these laws. The joy of the creative phase influences
even the darkest aspects of the destructive, for when the
greater truth enters into its lesser parts, no part is simple or
final. Thus we may see death at the center of life, yet likewise life perpetually triumphant over death; and those who
live according to this vision shall become, at last, infinitely
wise and eternally whole.

A Ceremony for the First Day of the Year

Here begins the new flight of Earth about the Sun, the two risen together anew from the ashes of the past to carry life into the universe again. Out of darkness, into darkness, their light stands here rekindled for another enactment of the eternal cycle.

Before sunrise of this day, in a room facing the east, all its windows heavily curtained, the altar should be prepared. Cover it with a smooth, white cloth. Set three white candles at its center, and before them arrange these three things: a white bowl holding crushed ice, a triangular prism of clear glass, and a mortar full of pure white chalk ground to a dust. At one end of the altar place a vessel containing oil of gardenia, and before it a white bird's feather. At the other end, a clear goblet full of white mint liqueur. All garments worn, robes and the like, should be white, with no embellishment save for a solar amulet which may hang about the neck.

The time of sunrise must be determined beforehand; then, at this moment, the ceremony shall begin.

First light the candle behind the mortar full of chalk, saying:

> *I am the light of all days that are passed, and my name*
> *is **preparation**.*

Then light the candle behind the bowl of ice, saying:

> *I am the light of this day today, and my name is **renewal**.*

Then light the candle behind the prism, saying:

> *I am the light of all days to be, and my name is*
> ***revelation**.*

When the candles are lighted, the mortar of chalk should be lifted in both hands, and this said:

> *Ancient earth turned to stone,*
> *Whitened dust of ancient bone,*
> *Pure as death, cold as snow,*
> *Dead thou wast, but livest now.*

The chalk should then be poured out over the ice, and these words said:

> *Crystal crushed, vision broken,*
> *Water fettered, words unspoken,*
> *What is frozen shall be warm,*
> *What is formless shal take form,*
> *What was scattered shall be whole,*
> *Given life within this bowl.*

Then with both hands mix the chalk and ice in the bowl until a milky substance is formed. The fingers so whitened should then be pressed for some moments to the brow of every person present, each time with these words:

> *This purifies thee as it is pure*
> *This gives thee life as it is given life*
> *The past prepares thee*
> *The present renews thee*
> *To thee the future shall be revealed.*

The oil of gardenia should then be poured, a spoonful or so, into the palm of the left hand, and an anointment of all three candles performed, thus: dip up this oil with the bird's feather, and brush it over the sides of the candles until the wax is scented and shining, upon which, this should be said:

> *White of petals, white of ice,*
> *White of dust and white of stone,*
> *White of wax and white of glass,*
> *White of crystal, white of bone,*
> *All things keeping, all things giving,*
> *Out of nothing, all things living,*
> *Out of emptiness, all light,*
> *Out of blindness, now our sight.*

The goblet of liqueur should then be held up to each candle in turn, that the flames may shine through it; afterwards, it should be passed for every person to drink, until it is emptied.

The prism should then be raised in both hands high above the head, and these words spoken:

> *I am the white sun risen out of darkness:*
> *From my brow springs all life again and again.*
> *I am now prepared, I am now renewed,*
> *I am now thy hope, and thy covenant, and thy revelation.*

The window curtains should quickly be drawn aside, and the prism held up to the Light. If the day be fair and unclouded, the Sun's early rays may be caught in the prism and cast into the room; if there be clouds, the brightest part of the sky should be gazed upon through the prism's side; then also should the feather be held up and gazed upon through the prism, that it may be seen tinged with spectral color. After which, these words should be spoken:

> *The sun is living; he is risen;*
> *The white bird ascends, and we ascend;*
> *Out of the whitened ashes of winter,*
> *Out of the white stone and the white crystal,*
> *Out of the pure white flame;*
> *His feathers are scarlet and they are azure,*
> *They are fiery, they are verdant,*
> *They are golden, and they are of royal purple;*
> *He is all things living,*
> *He is the spring and the summer,*
> *He is the autumn and the winter,*
> *He is time, he is revelation,*

He burns from this first dawn
Even unto the last darkness of the year
Into which he will fall
And from which he will rise again
And from which he will rise again
And from which he will rise again.

Then the prism may be replaced upon the altar, and the candles blown out, with these final words:

These go out
But not the sun:
We do not end
What has begun.

So shall the ceremony be brought to its conclusion.

A Ceremony for Mid-February ❧

⁕ At the time when one is most weary of winter's cold
and emptiness, then shall this ceremony be directed toward
the fertile promises of Earth and the warmth hidden in her
patient flesh. For she sleeps only, and her awakening has
been assured by the fires of December and by the newly
arisen light of January. At the Vernal Equinox will she truly
turn to new conception. Yet even now in this spare-seeming
month, her substance is complete, her wealth immense, and
by proper invocation there may be found a softening in her
stony frosts. Call forth then the strength of her darkened
seeds, and behold her no longer barren but only bared, soon
to be summoned by the Sun of spring.

The altar for this ceremony should be spread with a
length of brown velvet. Six candles, colored as the six colors
of the spectrum, shall be set in a row, according to the spectrum's order, along the cloth. No incense or scent of any sort
should be provided, but all garments worn shall be ornate
and fantastical, with flowing scarves and ribbons of gaudy
hues, many bright amulets and strands of beads, and rings
upon the fingers and the toes (for the feet should be bare).
Some budded twigs, rinsed clean and set in an earthen jug of
water, should be placed at one end of the altar, and at the
other a like jug holding new golden ale, with an earthen
mug beside it. In the center of the table should stand a large
pottery bowl half-filled with Earth dug up that day from

the cold garden, and near it a small box of seeds, either of flowers or from any common weed, as burdock, which stands even now in the waste places, full of fertile knots and burrs. The time of day for this ceremony is not important, yet it might best be performed in the early evening following some afternoon of Sun and moderate thaw.

Thus all shall begin—the six candles are lighted, and these words said:

> *Earth asleep in winter's bed,*
> *On thy limbs this light be shed,*
> *On thy face as still as stone*
> *And silent, dreaming of the sun:*
> *He shall come to claim his own,*
> *Thou shalt waken to him soon*
> *Yet today with candle beams*
> *We ourselves may warm thy dreams.*

Each candle in turn should be passed over the bowl of Earth, and then the bowl lifted in both hands, with these words:

> *Flowers of sun*
> *Flowers of earth*
> *Sleeping, turn*
> *To share our breath.*

Set down the bowl and remove the twigs from the jug of water. Hold them over the bowl a few moments, then stand them upright in the jug of ale, saying:

> *Now may this golden potion of the sun*
> *Fill thee with sweetness and a brightened sleep*
> *Wherein thy dreams shall wear a better shape*
> *To set thee flowering when thy sleep is done.*

Then take the jug of water and pour it over the Earth in the bowl until all the Earth is moistened. Each person should now bend over this bowl, and breathe upon it thrice, while these words are recited thrice:

> *Warmth of our breath warm thy breath,*
> *Warmth of our flesh warm thy flesh:*
> *We who are waking melt thy stone,*
> *We who are living thaw thy bone:*
> *Into thy spirit we breathe ours:*
> *Out of thy sleep we father flowers.*

Next scatter upon the surface of the watered Earth all the seeds from the box, with these words:

> *Sparks, stars, suns, seeds,*
> *Soon be raised to glorious weeds,*
> *Noble roses, sovereign trees,*
> *All whose strength begins in these.*

Take then the twigs from the jug of ale, set them again in the other jug, and fill the earthen mug with ale; it should be offered to all present, with this:

> *Where life has stood*
> *The draught is good*

So drink the brew
And live anew.

When the ale is finished all should attend to these words:

Now the sleeper dreams her golden dream,
Bound in warmth that flickers ever brighter:
Yet we may surround her quiet bed,
Her limbs she rests in subtle nakedness,
With all the gaudy garments we have kept
To drive dark winter back into the grave.
She sleeps in nothing but her fertile flesh
To shield her from the wind and winter's evil,
Then should we hide our everlasting heat
Behind the colors of all spring and summer?
Cast off those coverings and be
No less prepared to greet the sun than she.

Each one should then take off some articles of bright clothing and ornament, much or little according to inspiration,
and all these be piled before the altar as an offering. Say then:

This is our warmth
To earth now offered,
These our flowers
Plucked for her taking:
We her attendants
Wait for her waking,
So we may rise,
Like her, well favored

> *By sun and his strength*
> *Through all his reign's length.*

All should then bend in obeisance over the bowl wherein
earth, water, and seeds are contained, each saying:

> *I offer thee only*
> *What is thine:*
> *I am thy seed*
> *And thy creation*
> *So may I grow*
> *And so remain*
> *Thine image, spirit,*
> *Flesh, and vision.*

The ceremony shall then be ended by each person's breaking a fragment of twig from those in the jug to keep for a
talisman and covenant.

A Ceremony for the Vernal Equinox 🌿

🌿 As on this day the Sun returns to strength and Earth is roused from her fast sleep, all the signs of her awakening shall proclaim this glad event, and great rejoicing attend their nuptials.

Thus, in the late evening of this day, the altar shall be covered in a fair cloth of bright yellow, and twelve yellow candles be set upon it in a single row. No flowers should decorate the altar, but it is of great importance that many long withes of the willow tree, bound with yellow ribbon into a sheaf, be laid out upon the cloth. A brass bell, incense of sandalwood, oil or a balm, also of sandalwood, a vessel of sweet golden wine, and a goblet, should all be arranged before the candles. As for robes and the like, they shall be all of yellow, light and falling free about the body. Little adornment is desired, other than plain gold rings upon the fingers.

As the ceremony begins, the room should still remain in darkness. The bell is sounded once, and then the first of the twelve candles is lighted, with these words, spoken softly:

> *What is this sound*
> *And what this light,*
> *Bringing an end*
> *To sleep and night?*

The bell is rung again, and another candle lighted, which two things are thus repeated until all twelve candles have been lit. Say, then, less softly:

Whence this music?
Whose this flame?
Who wakes earth
To life again?

The bound willow withes are then grasped firmly in their center, and the cut ends rapped thrice upon the altar; these words shall follow:

Who is it knocks,
Who would come in?
She knows him still
Her lord, **the sun!**

The incense then is lighted, and oil or balm taken to anoint the hands, arms, and faces of all who attend. Thereafter, this is said:

Let her prepare
Her flesh most fair
For his desire
Whose flesh is fire.

Next one of the candles is carried to the door of the room, and these words spoken:

Unbolt the door
For he is here:
Now lead him forth
To greet his earth.

Open the door, then slowly move back to the altar. Set the candle down again, and speak these lines:

> *Now the youthful sun doth enter*
> *Once again his dear earth's chamber:*
> *Golden flames proclaim her lover,*
> *Soft she wakes beneath his fervor,*
> *Strong he shines in amorous fever*
> *Quick to win her passion's favor,*
> *Fire to fire they cleave together,*
> *Kindling spring, conceiving summer,*
> *Joined forever and forever*
> *Though dark autumn come, and winter.*

Take the willows next and undo the ribbon that binds them. The two ends of a single withe should be wound together to form a circlet, and then others likewise fashioned, one to be placed upon the head of everyone present. When this has been done, speak these words:

> *As withes are yellow the willow shall bring*
> *Gold for queen earth, and gold for her king:*
> *A sheaf and a crown and a round wedding ring,*
> *For this is the song that the willow doth sing:*
> *"O yellow the sun that shall turn me to green,*
> *And yellow his fires that burn for my queen,*
> *Yellow my branches that marry the twain*
> *Till I weave them a cradle of green leaves and rain."*

Then the crowns shall be unwound, and all the wands laid end to end about the floor in a great circle. Let all present now step within this circle, to stand in a ring while this is said:

> *This the circle of the sun,*
> *This the circle of the earth,*
> *This the circle of his flame,*
> *This the circle of her faith.*
> *A circle of gold, a crown of fire,*
> *Turned to the circle of their desire.*
> *A pledge of love, a marriage ring,*
> *To bind the queen, to bind the king.*

Next a libation of wine should be poured into the goblet and drunk by each person, with these words:

> *Here at the marriage*
> *Of sun and earth*
> *Drink to them both*
> *Eternal health.*

The goblet should be refilled and drunk until the wine is gone. Then all shall say:

> *Bride and bridegroom*
> *Bound together,*
> *Bind us too*
> *To one another.*

Half the number of those present shall then each take a

willow withe from the floor and with it encircle the waist of another celebrant, while these words are said:

> *We are the sun,*
> *We are the earth,*
> *Circles of fire,*
> *Circles of flesh.*
> *Spring is our marriage,*
> *Spring is our bed,*
> *So in this spring*
> *Our souls are wed.*
> **Joined forever and forever**
> **Though dark autumn come, and winter.**

The couples should then embrace, and the candles be blown out; thus the ceremony is concluded. Any true marriages that arise from this ritual shall be known supremely favored and not easily undone.

A Ceremony for the New Moon in April 🌱

🌒 When the first crescent Moon of April is setting at
evening, go out and gather from the trees some of their small
branches, budded or in new leaf. Bring them in and set them
in a clear glass jar of water. Then the altar may be prepared.

Cover it with a cloth of bright green, and set two green
candles at either end; arrange at the altar's center the jar of
branches. A silver goblet and a flask containing green mint
cordial mixed equally with white juniper spirits should be
placed to one side of the branches, and, on the other side, a
green balm of myrrh and vetiver combined. The clothing
should be simple, of both green and white, worn with necklace and rings of silver that should be neither weighty nor of
crude design. Some small silver amulet bearing the image of
the crescent Moon would be most fitting.

The ceremony shall begin with these words:

> *Lucina*
> *Lucina*
> *Occidua*
> *Sed nunc orior*
> *Natio, natio!*

Light the candles, and then turn, with the arms held out
wide and curved upward, to say this:

> *Crescent lucina,*
> *Sunk in the west,*

Born this night,
Mother of mothers,
Mother of waters
Mother of green leaves,
Cup of silver, cup of green waters,
Holding the waters of sky,
Holding the waters of birth,
Holding the waters of sea,
Holding the waters of earth,
Bear us these leaves,
Bear us this season,
Bear us the green child
Who shall be thy child,
Who shall be our child,
Who shall be ourselves.

Next kneel down, and say these words:

Thou who are Lucina
Thou who are Diana
Thou who are light
Thou who livest in darkness
Thou who createst
Thou who destroyest
Thou who changest ever
From life to death
And from death to life,
Hide now thy face of cold fury,

> *Ready thy warm womb of mercy,*
> *Quench thy cold white fire*
> *In the warm green waters of spring.*
> *We shall become thy children,*
> *Therefore be thou our mother,*
> *Now in the season of mercy,*
> *Now in the season of birth.*

Then rise, and take the green balm, to anoint first the candles and next the hands and faces of all present, saying:

> *April is ever a green season,*
> *The season of the green child:*
> *Who now shall see him*
> *Springing from the waters of the womb?*
> *From the womb of the moon,*
> *From the womb of the earth,*
> *From the womb of green April,*
> *Who shall see him*
> *Where he springs forth?*
> *Here he shall be seen,*
> *Here he shall be born,*
> *Here he shall be revealed.*

Remove the branches from the jar of water, and raise them high for all to see. Then lay them down, tenderly, as with an infant, upon the altar, and say this:

> *Here is the moon's babe*
> *Born now to all of us.*

He is our green child,
He is our brother and our son.
What is his name?
His name is given by the earth,
His name is given by water,
His name is given by us,
His name is our name:
*His name is **Life**.*

Here take the jar of water, and with the fingers of the right hand sprinkle drops from it upon the branches. Then turn, holding the jar, and sprinkle further drops upon the face of each attendant, with these words:

*I name thee **Life***
After this child
*Whose name is also **Life**,*
Whose mother is the moon,
Whose mother is water,
Whose mother is the earth,
Whose mother is ever thy mother.

Then take the flask of green potion, and fill the goblet. Let each person drink from it, passing it until it shall be empty, and then say:

We have drunk the green waters of the moon,
We have seen the offspring of her mercy.
She has delivered us from the cold fire of her face,
She has borne us from the warm waters of her womb.

We are her green children,
We are delivered and born
*And we are given the name of **Life**,*
As all green things now are named,
As all things now are born anew.

The candles may now be blown out and the ceremony ended. But the branches must afterwards be replaced in the jar of water and carefully kept until their leaves have opened fully, and later withered. Then they should be strewn about some ploughed field, that their substance may continue perpetually fruitful.

A Ceremony for the First of May 🌸

🌿 For this Ritual of Affirmation, performed best in full sunlight or even out of doors, the altar should bear two deep blue candles upon a cloth of paler blue. About the candles a profusion of blue and near-blue flowers should be strewn—

the blue violet, hyacinth and grape hyacinth, blue flag, wisteria, periwinkle, forget-me-not, scilla, or any others then in bloom. No incense should be necessary, but the candles may be anointed beforehand with oils of hyacinth and lilac.

Provide also a potion of violets, prepared thus: one day earlier pour boiling water over two handfuls of violet blossoms, to fill a small stone jar, and preserve this mixture in a cool place until shortly before the ceremony. At that time, strain the liquor into a goblet of clear glass, stir into it two spoonfuls of honey until they are dissolved, and so it may be set upon the altar.

The garments for this ceremony should be all of blue, pale, deep, or of various shades, and glittering ornaments of gold, silver, and crystal should be worn as well.

To begin the rites, light the candles and say:

Sprung from the dark into the light,
Behold these flames of blue.
Most innocent, most intense,
Released from the depths of night,
Leached from the pale bones of winter,
Formed in the matrix of earth,
Risen in the fires of the sun,
Fed by the waters of spring.
Now they burn, now they ascend as wings of blue flame,
Aspiring to that azure realm whither all flesh aspires,
Where all growth shall find its perfect form.

Yet even now these are perfect:
They offer us their existence as a sign of present perfection,
That we may believe in the flesh even here,
Even beneath the realm of the spirit
Where final perfection must dwell.
For though they aspire to the heavens,
Yet they remain most earthly:
Here they live as we must live,
In the realm of the flesh—and yet they are perfect,
And today we celebrate this moment for all flesh
As it stands for an instant balanced,
Poised perfectly between heaven and earth.

The potion of violets should be held up, and these words spoken over it:

The spirit of blue violets
Is the spirit of the flesh:
Earth and sky together blended,
Two realms fused and infused,
Of whose two springs we may drink
Without violence to either
Nor to either one neglect.
So may we be wholly glad,
So may we stand still
While our feet take root upon the earth
In harmony with flowers and with trees,
The deep roots and the long boughs:

So may we stand winged,
Feathers spread, weightless
With all earth's glories
Wreathed about our veins,
Garlanded about our mortal limbs:
So may we drink the elixir
Of earth and heaven, and be glad,
As we are mortal and immortal,
Fixed here in motionless ascent,
Turned perfect in this moment,
Perfect in this perfection of flesh,
Drinking the elixir of perfection.

All should drink from the goblet, and then stand with arms upraised, while this is said:

The tree knows the sky,
Touching it with ascending leaves:
The tree holds the sky
Lightly in good green leaves:
As its light leaves drink the sky
The tree becomes our spirit,
As now the leaves of our spirit
May dance upon their boughs of flesh.

One of the celebrants should then move to stand before the altar, and the others shall take the flowers from it and wreathe the person with them, fixing their stems into the hair, over the ears, upon the shoulders, about the clothing, and shall last fill the hands with violets. Any flowers that remain may be scattered about the feet, and then these words are said:

> *O man who standest as a tree,*
> *Taller even than all these flowers,*
> *How should we not worship thee*
> *Whose flesh is the flesh of stars?*
> *Where thou growest there are gardens,*
> *Where thou shinest there is sight:*
> *Though thou fallest from such season*
> *Into winter, into night,*
> *Yet thine ills this day are healed,*
> *And they faults we here deny*
> *Stand this instant here revealed*
> *Perfect scion of earth and sky.*

Every person should then touch the head and the feet of the one who stands garlanded, and then, kneeling, receive one of the violets from that person's hands, who shall then say:

> *Receive this sign,*
> *The perfect flower,*
> *Token given*
> *Of this hour:*
> *Though its petals*
> *Pale and wither,*
> *What we worship*
> *Lives forever.*

All shall then rise, and the candles be extinguished to end the ceremony. Each should afterwards carefully preserve the violet given, for its powers shall not pass away.

A Ceremony for the Summer Solstice 🌿

🌿 The Ritual of High Solar Celebration should be performed at true noon upon this day. Even if the Sun should be obscured by unfavorable weather, these rites shall well invoke the spirit of his rays; or, if the Sun does indeed shine, that spirit shall be the more evidently enhanced and glorified.

The altar should be covered with a cloth of gold, and a single gold candle be set upon it. Before this candle should be placed a large brass bowl filled with Earth, having strewn upon its surface some glowing embers of charcoal. Arrange elsewhere upon the altar these things: a vase of bunched daisies and buttercups; a small dish of powdered frankincense and orrisroot, well blended; a vial holding tincture of ambergris; a flask of fine brandy and a goblet; and, finally, a long golden ribbon, to which have been tied many small gold bells along its length.

There should also be provided a young tree, slender, yet the height of a man, or some goodly full bough cut from a greater tree, having equal height, and this arranged to stand upright against the altar at one end.

The robes for this ceremony should be of gold, or else of white profusely decorated with gold patterning and solar emblems. Tied to each wrist should be several gold ribbons, near an ell in length, and about the neck chains of gold should hang, or gilded solar amulets, or necklaces of amber, while the fingers should bear many and various gold rings. Each person in attendance should wear upon the head a gilded coronet (fashioned from wire, metallic paper, or other appropriate materials) from the back of which shall hang further gold ribbons like those at the wrists.

Have a small clock that strikes brought into the ceremonial chamber, and shortly before noon all celebrants shall stand waiting, in silence, until it has struck the hour. Following the last stroke, the candle shall be lighted, with these words:

Now sun stands at the year's zenith,
And his manifold creations throng before him:
Hear then their words:

King of seasons, tower of light,
Tree of fire, crest of flight,
Eternal flower, crown of flame,
Golden apex, summer's name,
Sun our ruler, sun our lover,
Sun our father, sun our brother,
Where thou shinest from thy throne
Burn away our mortal bone,
Turn our flesh to breathless air,
Bid us rise to meet thee there:
Where our spirits share thy reign
Nor fall to mortal life again.

Cast then a handful of the powdered incense upon the
coals, and say:

So sun, may we like these vapors,
Freed from substance,
Drawn by fire to essential spirit,
Rise above our frail and vulnerable compounds,
Seeking thy kingdom of the immortal spirit:
For are we not thine heirs,
Fathered upon earth by thy gold rays?
Are we not fire of thy fire
Kindled in the same universal dark?

Wherefore then should we not rise with thee,
To stand upon thy right hand,
Where all things stand immortal,
Where every spirit burns eternal?
And lo, we are winged with the wings of thy summer,
Sprung from earth
As thy bright fathering rays have called us forth:
Lo, on the flames of spring have we aspired toward thee,
And on the wings of summer now we rise,
On thy wings who are the father of all wings:
Thy winged sphere our kingdom,
Whither we ascend,
Where we shall find our immortality
Beyond time and space:
The fires of thy face and the fires of thy name
Shall be our own transfiguration and redemption.

Then over the coals a little brandy should be poured, and as it burns, these words said:

Now we shall arise,
Now we shall ascend,
Now we are assumed
In the greater fire
Of thy golden sphere,
O perfect golden king,
Never now to die,
Never to descend,

Nor to be consumed:
Now our wings are fixed
In thy heart of amber,
Now our faces fixed
In thine eye of flame,
Now our names recorded
In this single moment,
Evermore to burn
As everlasting brands
Upon the endless dark.

Brandy should be then poured to fill the goblet, and all should drink thereof, while this is spoken, for each:

Fire of the spirit,
Elixir of the sun,
Fill us and preserve us
While we burn as one.

Then the tree or bough should be taken and held upright before the altar, that with the tincture of ambergris it may be anointed, trunk and twig and leaf. Then anoint the hands of every celebrant, and let this dialogue be performed between the leader and all the others (who shall ask the questions, the leader answering):

What is this fair tree?
It is the tree of sun.
From what land doth it rise?
It riseth from the earth.

How high shall it grow?
To this moment's zenith.
When shall its leaves wither?
Never shall they wither.
Even in the autumn?
Even in the winter.
Whom shall it raise up?
Thou it raiseth up.
By what noble power?
By the sun's great fire.
How shall we attend it?
Crown it and adore it.
Crown it as a king?
Crown it as yourselves.
Shall it then live always?
Thou shalt then live always.
Who shall give us life?
The sun shall give thee life.
Yet who redeems the sun?
Thou redeemest sun.
How do we redeem him?
Thy vision doth redeem him.
What shall be our vision?
What is seen this moment.
What is seen this moment?
This tree, adorned and crowned.

Each person shall then remove the coronet from his or her head, and hang it upon a twig of the tree, also weaving the gold ribbons among its leaves. When all have done this, speak these words:

> *Now the tree is leaved with gold,*
> *Now the sun receives his crown,*
> *Now our deaths are left below*
> *And we stand beside his throne:*
> *Who can say that we shall fall*
> *When the earth must turn away?*
> *Who shall make our mortal fate*
> *On the surface of this day?*
> *Who may call our vision folly*
> *While we look upon its face?*
> *Sun shall turn the bells of fools*
> *To gold, in his eternal grace.*

Here grasp the string of bells in both hands, and hold it up for all to see, saying:

> *For as the laughter of gold bells is a joy to fools,*
> *So the reign of the gold sun rings joy*
> *Down all the silent halls of space,*
> *Where only the dead deny it,*
> *The dead who have neither eyes nor ears:*
> *For only we have said, as fools have said,*
> ***There is no death, we shall not die,***
> *Yet who but those who say so*
> *Shall be called immortal?*

> *Though gold bells may laugh*
> *For fools alone to dance to,*
> *Yet where is dancing in the tomb*
> *Or laughter in the grave?*
> *Then wear the bells of laughter,*
> *Dance the dance of life,*
> *That in the silent dark*
> *Death shall be mocked, and rave.*

The bells should be shaken thrice, and then wound among the leaves of the tree. Next say this:

> *Crowned with gold,*
> *Wreathed in joy,*
> *Art thou merely*
> *Summer's toy?*
> *No, thou teachest*
> *Laughter higher*
> *Than the halls*
> *of death inspire:*
> *Though we face*
> *And while we fail,*
> *We may laugh,*
> *And laughing, fall.*
> *What is wound*
> *About the sun*
> *May in no way wise*
> *Be undone;*
> *Though the seasons*

Cloud his reign,
Still we find him
Free from stain:
Fallen even
Into ruin,
He shall stand
As now we see him:
Crowned with gold,
Wreathed in joy,
Substance death
Shall not destroy.

The tree should then be grasped by all, and shaken thrice, that its bells may ring loudly. Then the candle may be extinguished. Afterwards, the tree should be borne away into the midst of a wood, and left there in all its adornment. That place, now sacred, must never be revisited by any of those who accompanied it there.

A Ceremony for Late July 🌿

🌿 This ceremony, which is performed in recognition of the dark side of the year, should begin well after sunset. The altar is draped with several lengths of the heaviest and richest fabrics, velvets, thick satins, and the like, in various shades of dark red and purple. Six candles of a reddish purple color should be set upon it, and before them should be ranged a wine glass for each celebrant. On one side place a great jug containing the libation, sweet dark red wine mixed equally with blackberry brandy, having a pinch of ground cumin seed sprinkled on its surface. At the other end of the altar should stand a vase of the deepest red roses, strongly perfumed.

Wound all among these things, also trailing down from the altar, all manner of vines should be arranged—of the grape, of purple clematis, of woodbine, of moonflower, or any others suitably long and leafy. A flask of mixed oils—rose, patchouli, and lavender should be placed near the vase of roses, and also a small vial of that tincture known as gentian violet.

The celebrants should be clothed in as little as possible, with a few long, thin scarves of purple taking the place of any outer robes on this occasion—some heavy rings, also earrings, of brass or dull gold, and about the neck some amulet betokening passion or fertility shall be worn for ornament.

Let the candles be lighted to begin the ritual, and these words be said:

We who have attained all life
Now ask still further joy:
For what is sovereignty that turns aside from pleasure,
What is power that it may stand still and rest content?
Having flown from flesh to spirit,
Having laughed at death,
Should we not rejoice even in the realm
Where flesh and death prevail?
Turned invincible, we may descend upon
Our conquered lands and claim our spoil.
Where we have lived before, fixed to earth,
We now may live again:
Thus, with new strength,
As the long vine that hangs upon the tree of life,
We wind our wisdom home again
And seize what we have won.
Night shall be our drinking hall,
No longer held by death and his dull minions:
Crowd them out, those joyless hordes who will not laugh,
And pour the wine of victory!
As we have conquered blood,
Now blood we shall enjoy!

Here pour out the libation from the jug into every goblet,
and let each drink the draught and fill his or her glass again
until the face grows flushed, the eye brilliant. While all shall
drink, this is to be recited:

Upon the hills and in the forests
Now the trees and vines are warm and full of leaves:
And lo! the tree of life, the tree of sun,
Is crowned with golden vines in the wood
Where we have hidden it:
Hidden in the darkness of the grove,
It stands where late we set it,
And its golden vines are full
Of purple flowers, purple fruit:
Shall we not return into that grove
And pluck the fruit that should be ours?
Wherefore should we waste the joys great sun has given us,
Or fear the powers of our strengthened blood?
We are the living gods, heaven and earth are ours:
Let us then possess both kingdoms
Better than we knew to do before,
Let us learn to do now as we please.
For even sun has weakened now, his zenith fails,
His gold meridian sinks and falters down the air,
And he is lord of what has been, not of what is.
But we, but we, are lords of everywhere:
We rule the darkness and the light,
And will do what we will.
That tree of life, that tree of sun,
Upholds us where we grasp as vines
And take their limbs our prisoners.
All things we hold,

And we shall not release the branches full of purple fruit
Until we have been filled:
We fill, we swell, we are the purple of the deepest rose,
The purple of the royal vine, now filled with wine
And grown as great as all the whole great universe—
Its infinite purple fruit, its darkest flower ripe,
Its heavy petals folded full about the sun's gold heart.
Let us swallow the sun, whole, in our universal orb,
Ourselves the cosmic purple globe where lo!
The sun has shrunk to nothing but a silver seed.
Lo! we have swallowed up the sun, and we expand,
We now encompass all, and all, and all.

The flask of oil shall now be passed around to all, that each may pour out a little into one palm. Then each shall anoint another, hands and face and limbs, while this is said:

Let us glorify our flesh,
Let us celebrate our bounty
And the sweetness of our flowering.
For we are yet the flowering of all the universe,
Yea, even so we are its flesh and blood and fruit.
Who shall stay our hands when they would act,
And who shall starve our mouths when we would feast?
Gods we live, and none may call us mortal:
Save for the dry and lipless mouth of death,
But where is death?
We see him not, we recognize him not.

Even if he should gnaw the root beneath the earth,
Even while he gnaws the hidden root
That binds the tree of sun to earth,
The tree of sun where in we climb and feast on life,
Even while he gnaws the root and starves the vein,
The fruit is ours: and lo!
We see him not, neither are we blind.
It is but wine that veils our eyes, and wine is life,
We only drink what is our own:
Wherefore should it blind us?
We see ourselves, and this shall be enough of sight.
For O, sweet, ourselves are sweet,
Our every self as sweet as flowers and sweet fruit:
We hold the wine of all the great sweet universe,
And of this wine we drink,
We draw all sweetness from the tree of life.
Whose blood may then be drained?
Death's blood alone,
And not the tree's wherein we climb rejoicing.
Sweet, sweet, our own dark blood,
As we are filled with life.
Let us drink up sweetest life with our dark lips,
Let us cleave unto the heart of life and suck its juice,
Let us kiss the heart, the vein, the hand of life
Whence all our highest sweetness springs.

Here each celebrant should kiss the left palm of another.

Then all shall come forward to the altar and receive on their left palms a drop of the gentian violet, after which the hand should be clenched and opened again and the violet marks be allowed to dry. Let these words next be recited, while each time with the words: *"Put out the candles,"* one candle should be duly extinguished, until all are dark.

> *Now we are marked with the wine and the blood,*
> *Now we are marked with the fruit and the flower,*
> *Now we are marked with our lust and our power.*
> *So let this mark be a sign to death:*
> *That laughter is stronger than mourning,*
> *That blindness is more radiant than sight,*
> *That excess is nobler than abstinence,*
> *That pride is stronger than meekness.*
> *We shall not lie with death in the sober grave*
> *While there is life with whom to lie,*
> *And to drink, and to celebrate:*
> *Better to lie upon earth, drunk with excess*
> *With the glories of flesh and blood,*
> *Better to kiss and be marked by kisses of flowering blood,*
> *Even if they should wound us,*
> *Even if they should drain our veins to death-white ropes,*
> *Even if they betray us and deliver us*
> *Into the knotted bone-white bonds of death.*
>
> *We shall dare even to put out the candles now,*
> *And drink the darkness.*

O put out the candles, then, and
Kiss the darkness of blood:
But call it never the darkness of death,
For we have refused all death:
Call it the darkness of life,
For we go blind, and admit no darkness
But living darkness.

Put out the candles now,
Even while we grow blind, and we do not see,
And we insist that we will not see.

Put out the candles, and we shall embrace the darkness,
We shall insist upon darkness, kissing in darkness,
Living forever in darkness, our flesh and our blood
And our wine as dark as all darkness itself.

Put out the candles,
Give us even the darkness of death,
That we may make love to death
And warm him with blood and wine,
And cover his bones with kisses,
And turn him to flesh and blood
In the tyranny of our sweetest darkness
Of flesh and blood.

Put out the candles!

Thus in darkness shall this ritual be consummated, and so ended.

A Ceremony for Mid-August ❦

❧ Near the middle of August when nights reveal the meteors of Perseus, proceed at sunset to cover the altar with a cloth of pale orange silk. Set thereon five candles of orange color, and to one side of them, in an aged and rusting container, some twigs whose leaves have begun to fade or brown, also stalks of the stinging nettle and of those plants named Artemisia, the pale-leaved wormwood. On the other side place a small cup of brown vinegar in which has been mixed some dark and bitter vermouth. Next, in the center of the altar set an earthen bowl full of dust gathered from the roadside, and upon the surface of this dust a long, silver ribbon coiled small.

The garments for this ceremony should be of dusty orange or rust-red. Only one fine silver chain may be worn about the neck, while the hands and feet should remain bare.

First the candles should be lighted, with these words:

> *Now sun tarnishes, his ruddy fire cools,*
> *Now haze and darkness veil his rusted gold:*

Soon stars will topple down the heavy sky,
Will headlong fall, flail their rays like giddy fools,
Fainting, drunken from all summer's draughts,
And fall with a muted chime, as of sad bells that fail:
Nor are these stars, but only motes of stars
Cast out from heaven, wated on the air,
Trailing themselves to meet mists before they die:
So bleeds the sun, in sparks of withered dust,
Not even spending blood, but drawn to drought:
A void whose deepest wound may yield
No more than dry chaff blown across a blighted field.

The silver ribbon should then be uncoiled from the bowl
and held out in both hands, with these words:

Our golden god slew once the dragon of the dark
And led his bride, the earth, out from her stony chains:
Proud he ascended to the sky's fixed pinnacle,
And nothing crossed his love, nor dared his winged fire,
Yet now her face of worship cools to sullen stars,
Now from the waving summer forests of her hair
The gold leaves fall, and sudden serpents wind their knots
About those roots, and venoms taint the swollen air:
He falls, he cracks, he weeps, his stony meteors shower
Down their dust, cold as the silver serpent's glare.

The ribbon should then be wound about the hands and
wrists, and this said:

For the pale serpent has wounded sun's poor heel
Where late he flew so fair on winged feet:
Well hidden in the dust, that clever tongue
Forked whetted words into his golden flesh:
Dark wisdom of the deust, that can but kill,
How shall we learn to heal the sovereign ill?

The ribbon should then be knotted about the left wrist, and these words spoken:

There is no remedy for him, no remedy for us,
For we have shared his golden throne,
And we must share his fall:
His sovereignty now rusted to an arid rain of stars
Plummets us with him: we are bound to him at the wrist,
And at the heel, and at the heart: and where before
Those bonds were golden wreathes and golden vines,
Now they are cruel silver reins, leaving us silver scars,
Now they are coils of the silver serpent,
Knotted, and gray, and fierce.

Take up then the cup with its bitter potion, and let everyone present taste thereof, while these words are said:

Drink of his fallen blood,
Elixir venom-tainted,
Drink of his tarnished wine,
Wherein the sweet has fainted,
And shrunk to wormwood and to gall:
One taste brings death upon us all.

The ribbon should now be unknotted and spread full length upon the altar. Then the bowl of dust should be taken up and handfuls from it showered over the ribbon, with these words:

> *Down from his wound the universal dust*
> *Falls upon earth, and meets our further drought,*
> *Where wisdom curls and glints beside the road*
> *In sly conspiracy, and scrawls its words*
> *For all to study, who must learn to die:*
> *O serpens modax*
> *Scio, cado, morior*

Then every person should stand before the altar and press between the palms first, the faded leaves, next, the sprigs of Artemisia, and last, the stinging nettles (that their hurtful mark may be set upon each who attends this ceremony). At the same time, these words should be slowly recited, again and again:

> *O serpens modax*
> *Scio, cado, morior*

Then all shall bow their heads, while the candles are extinguished to end the ritual.

A Ceremony for the Autumnal Equinox ❦

❧ On this first day of autumn, when Sun's weakened reign bends altogether to the sovereignty of darkness, the altar should be shrouded in ragged cloths, faded, and gray with dust and age. No candle should light it, neither should any flower adorn it, save for several dried stalks of old and withered thistles, their heads pale with silken down, held in a common glass jar. An oil or balm of rue, bitter in scent, should be placed at one end of the altar; a thickly smoking incense, heavy and pungent, at the other; and at the center a clock, whose ticking is slow and resonant. Before the clock, set an empty wooden box, drab and scarred, fit only to be cast aside, holding within it an ordinary tumbler of cold water.

All garments must be old, worn and thin, as pale and tattered as can be found, and from the shoulders and the wrists torn rags instead of shawls or scarves shall hang; a veil of ragged gray should cover up the hair. No ornaments may deck the body, nor shall there be any color added to the face, nor sweet scent to the flesh.

At the moment when the Sun has set, stand before the altar and, in a low voice, say this:

Now the sun is overwhelmed,
And we are left alone to die:
With all the faded trees, the wasted flowers,
Do we also fade and waste.
Our birth, our youth, our prime,
Our proud excess, our cosmic fall:
Now ended all, and we are left
With the mean prize of poverty and dull decline,
To fill the silences between the ticks of time.
Whither fled our strength and our ascending leaves?
Whither fled our laughter and our foolish bells?
Where now stand those scaffoldings of fire,
Those limbs of light whereon we climbed,
Wherein we played?
All are now pulled down,
Our lean possessions shrunk to fill a little box:
And all our senses, our delights,
Turned pale and leached of taste,

Paled to a scentless draught
That rusts the heart to a mere foolish ticking clock.

All should then be silent and attend to the sound of the clock. After a short time, this shall be spoken softly, thrice over, in rhythm with the ticking:

The brain
Must break
The bone
Must crack
The blood
Must clot
The heart
Must stop
The flesh
Must rot.

Following this, all shall anoint their hands and faces with the oil of rue, and kneel upon the floor, with bowed heads, while this is said:

We are the stricken,
Dying of death,
Shrouded in weeds,
Wrapped in our loss:
Silent we wait,
Clouded by tears
Torn by the wind,

Ragged with mist:
Where we are wounded
There is no healing,
Where we decay
Nothing is sound,
Ravaged by night,
Abandoned by day,
Silent we wait,
Shadows of gray:
Old in our broken
Houses of flesh,
Old among ruined
Pillars of sun,
Old as the halls
To which we descend,
Old as this dark
That does not end.

Then let the tumbler of water be taken from the wooden box, and each person shall drink a little thereof, as this is said:

Elixirs fade
And potions fail,
The gold is rusted
From the grail,
The wine is changed
To water thin,
The blood is wasted

> *From the skin,*
> *And all that from*
> *This glass is drunk*
> *May leave us only*
> *Smaller shrunk.*

Then the jar of thistles shall be held up and this said over them:

> *Even the king*
> *Grows old and white*
> *When royal noon*
> *Has turned to night:*
> *Yet better the peace*
> *Of thistledown*
> *Than power under*
> *A thorny crown.*

Crush the thistles then into the wooden box, with these words:

> *Let him sleep*
> *His sleep of gray*
> *Where gold and purle*
> *Fall away,*
> *And let us lie*
> *Beside him here,*
> *Past pain or joy,*
> *Desire or fear.*

One celebrant shall cover this box of thistles with the veil from his or her head. Then that person shall come before the altar and say:

> *Shall there be no alternative?*
> *Neither recourse nor choice?*

Another shall answer:

> *The choice is sleep or madness:*
> *Go then, sleep that gray and silent sleep*
> *That comes before the silent dark,*
> *Warmed only by the poor domestic fire,*
> *That lean and flickering flame*
> *Lit upon the mortal hearth to comfort men in autumn:*
> *For it may warm, if not the spirit or the heart,*
> *And least the chilly fingers yet awhile.*

The first shall ask then:

> *Are these not the words of some gray serpent*
> *Flickering in the dust?*
> *Would it not be better to go mad and rave,*
> *To court the fair illusion of a greater fire?*

This shall be the answer:

> *Death is death, and even madness*
> *Should soon play us false.*
> *Better to sleep, better to close the curtains tight*
> *Against the treacherous laughter of the moon,*
> *And sleep with yet a little fire on the hearth:*

Then when the last tongue flickers and is gone,
The sleeper knows it not. Go now and sleep.

Thus shall the ceremony end, and all depart. The box of thistles later should be taken to some hearth fire, to be burned until only its ashes shall remain.

A Ceremony for the Full Moon in October ❦

❧ This ceremony is to be performed at night, although not so late as midnight. The altar should be spread with a silver cloth, and four silver candles set upon it. At the altar's center should stand numerous goblets, ringed about a black iron pot containing a block of ice and a large silver ladle. Before the pot set four vessels, each holding one of these: a pale white wine, a colorless cordial of anise flavor, white syrup of corn, and a dear extract of bitter almonds. At one end of the altar set a silver vase containing some naked twigs from the wild cherry tree, some dry stalks of burdock bearing numerous burrs, and a few briar canes, thorny and leafless. At the other end a round mirror, ten inches or so across, should lie upon the cloth, and beside it, these: a small silver bell, a spool of silver thread, and a small vial of jasmine oil.

The robes for this ceremony should be black, edged with silver and inscribed with designs of the Sun, Moon, and stars, all in silver. All manner of silver, diamond, or crystal ornaments should decorate the hands, wrists, neck, and ears, and silver ribbons may bind the hair. Even the eyelids and nails of the fingers should be silvered, and a single brilliant may be fixed at the center of the brow.

To begin the ceremony, the candles should be lighted and the silver bell rung four times. Then let this be said:

> *How should we cease from dying and from sleep*
> *Where we have taken refuge in deep silence?*
> *Doth death already rouse us with his music?*
> *No, death has naught to do with bells or music.*
> *This is a silver sound, a ghost of sound,*
> *An echo of some laughter we have known—*
> *Yet where is laughter, now that sun is gone?*
> *This is the sound of laughter changed to stone,*
> *And warmth to frost, and fire to reflection:*
> *O fearful ghost! It is the silver moon*

> *Whose mirror turns our deaths upon themselves:*
> *As the trapped creature gnaws his captive flesh,*
> *We waken into frenzy while we die.*

Let the mirror then be held up above the head for all to see, and these words recited by all:

> *Spirit of night,*
> *Spectre of sun,*
> *Scourge of the dying,*
> *Doom of the living,*
> *Egg of the serpent,*
> *Web of the spider,*
> *Servant of dreams,*
> *Lamp of delusion*
> *Beacon of evil,*
> *Bearer of power,*
> *Crystal of knowledge,*
> *Mirror of madness*
> *Art thou redemption?*
> *Art thou damnation?*
> *Shall we adore thee?*
> *Should we abhor thee?*
> *Bringest thou visions*
> *Of angels or demons?*
> *Shall we rejoice with thee in this awakening*
> *Or shall we fly from thee to kind death's comforting?*

Take the jasmine oil and anoint the candles, and also the
hands and brows of every celebrant, saying:

> *We live again*
> *And we are fair!*
> *The moon has risen*
> *Here to bear*
> *A mirror for*
> *Our altered faces,*
> *As their faded*
> *Flesh she chooses*
> *For her love*
> *That all things seizes.*
> *We are risen*
> *In her light,*
> *Where the dying*
> *Live again,*
> *These rags made whole*
> *And rearranged*
> *In patterns of*
> *Her ghostly chance*
> *What dulled and grayed*
> *Her light makes glitter,*
> *All our senses*
> *Wear her silver:*
> *Silver serpent,*
> *Silver spider,*

All show fair
Within her mirror.

Then over the ice in the iron cauldron, pour the contents of all four vessels, and stir them with the ladle to concoct the lunar libation, saying this:

Now her gift of fine confusion
Shall be strengthened in this potion:
Drink it, that her cold illusion
May redeem thy mortal vision.

The mixture should be ladled out into goblets for all to drink. After it has been consumed, this should be said:

Cold her kiss that breaks the brain to snow,
But fair her eyes where fire is white as crystal,
And fair her brow where sweet forgetfulness
Breaks as a sunrise, while she kills the sun.
We did not choose her madness, we were chosen:
Yet who would not prefer it to the dark?
We know no more of reason even there than now we do,
Where truth is so adorned by her elaborate threads
And crystals, woven about its form, that we forget its form:
Better her most dread hallucination
Than empty sleep where nothing shines or dances,
Better her dance of death, her panic throes,
Her tarantelle, than stillness in the grave,
And though her music leads us only there
We follow gladly all her dread diversions.

Then take the spool of silver thread, and tie its end to the silver bell. Let one person hold the bell tightly, while the thread is unreeled and wound about all other celebrants, back and forth among them, crossed and recrossed, until an irregular tangled web is formed, binding each within its pattern. Then say these words:

> *Bound in the silver web, be free;*
> *Dying in formless flame, now live:*
> *Maddened where madness is a joy,*
> *Fearful where fear is resurrection,*
> *Hold thou fast to this frail thread*
> *Until the last false light be shed.*
> *O moon, fair glory, ghost, and ghoul,*
> *What matter if we but feed thy evil:*
> *Art thou not a beauteous beast,*
> *And are we not better for beauty still?*
> *Let us at least be well betrayed*
> *And led to death by silver singing*
> *Rather than soft dispassionate night*
> *Where no sting blinds, no pain astounds,*
> *And even in anguish, no voice sounds.*

The bell shall then be rung continuously, while the silver thread is retraced among the celebrants and thus rewound upon its spool. The candles should finally be extinguished, but the bell should still ring until the last light is gone. Then shall the ceremony end.

A Ceremony for the Dark of the Moon ❧ *in November*

❧ For this ceremony, the altar must be covered with a plain black cloth of dull texture. Upon it set a single black candle, a large, flat, dark stone, a stick of white chalk, an incense burner containing some sharp-scented incense un-lighted, a box of ointment having a similar scent, and, final-ly, the whitened bone of an animal, this wrapped in a piece of black velvet. All garments worn must be of black entirely, with no adornment or decoration save for an amulet, bear-ing a death's-head, about the neck. A black shawl or hood should cover the head and shoulders of every person present.

At midnight the ceremony shall begin. First light the candle, then say these words:

The year grows dark
In the dark of the moon:

The mind grows dark
In the dark of the moon:
Nihil stat
Nihil stat
Nihil stat
Even the night is dead
Now at the dark of the moon:
Even the demons are dead
Now at the dark of the moon:
All who once lived are dead
Now at the dark of the moon:
Nihil stat
Nihil stat
Nihil stat
What shall remain?
This shall remain!

The bone should be quickly unwrapped and raised in both hands, to be contemplated in silence for several moments. Then these words are spoken:

Beneath the earth, behold the kingdom of the dead:
The place of darkness where no word is spoken,
Nothing moves:
And there the king of death sits always
On his carved black throne,
Sits there silent and unmoving, forever, and forever,
A ruler never challenged, never disobeyed:

A figure carved from bone, his face the face of silence,
Carved of death's own substance which is bone,
His eyes black shadows of silence, empty caves of bone.
He sits unmoving, while he rules absolutely by his silence
The vast hordes of the dead, those silent docile hordes
Ranked endlessly beneath the earth,
Silent figures of obedient bone.
Only one law rules their kingdom:
And it is carved deep upon the throne
Where sits eternally its maker and enforcer:
A single law, and one that is not broken
While the king of death rules silently forever and forever:
Carved in the stone above his silent and unmoving head,
*These words: **Thou shalt not live.***

The stone should then be raised by one celebrant for all to see, while with the chalk another shall write these same words upon it: ***Thou shalt not live.*** Then all shall chant this song of mortality:

Nor shall we live,
We who still live:
How shall we live
Where he is law?
Our life is death,
A downward path
Into the earth,
Where every breath
We dare to breathe

> *Is a farewell:*
> *Is a farewell:*
> *Is a farewell.*

The stone should now be replaced upon the altar, and the incense lighted, with these words:

> *Let us then praise thee, death,*
> *For thy law which is law,*
> *For thy power which is proven,*
> *For thy silence which is unbroken.*
> *Thou art past all sorrow and remorse,*
> *Thou art past change, and challenge, and failure:*
> *Thou art perfect, as darkness is perfection,*
> *Thou art perfect, while light may only flaw,*
> *Thou art perfect, as all else is imperfect,*
> *As even mighty madness is imperfect—*
> *Which we have learned, having ourselves been mad—*
> *And sun and moon are only flaws*
> *That flare and fade upon the perfect sphere*
> *Of thy eternal space and time:*
> *Let us then praise thee, death,*
> *Let us adore thy flawlessness*
> *Which shall become our own perfecton*
> *Who are imperfect now,*
> *Who shall yet become most perfect in thy law.*

The candle should now be anointed with the ointment, and the hands of all present anointed also. Then say:

Shall we now put out the candle?
Shall we now put out the candle?
Shall we now put out the candle?
There is nothing left to light,
Now at the dark of the moon,
Nothing to praise but death's kingdom,
Death's perfect universal dark,
Where there is no need for light.
And there we shall be made perfect,
There we shall learn all things,
Where there is no need for knowledge:
Nor need we speak a single word again,
*Not even ever more **farewell**:*
*Not even ever more **farewell**:*
*Not even ever more **farewell**.*

The candle should then be lifted from the altar, and blown out. Thus this ceremony is ended, as here the death of the year is made final and manifest.

A Ceremony for the Winter Solstice 🌿

❧ This ceremony bears the greatest significance of all during the year, resolving as it does the paradox of death and subsequent rebirth. So shall it be performed with utmost solemnity, yet also with highest rejoicing.

At some time before one o'clock in the morning of this day, the altar should be spread with a bright red cloth of rich material, such as velvet or heavy silk. Twelve red candles should be arranged in a circle at its center. In their midst set a golden basin full of ashes. At one end of the altar place a vase holding holly sprigs, fresh and full-berried, mixed with sprays of juniper and cedar; and at the other end, a flask of young red wine, with goblets sufficient for all who will attend the ceremony.

The robes should be also of red, but at the inception of the ceremony these should be covered up as much as possible by a wide black shawl or long cloak, worn over the head as well. All ornament and all decoration of the clothing should be of gold, but likewise worn well hidden as the ceremony begins.

When it is just one o'clock, the leader of the celebrants should be waiting outside the closed door to the ceremonial chamber, cloaked as has been prescribed, holding a lighted golden candle in a brass candlestick, and a bell of brass. The leader shall then ring the bell once, and one of the celebrants within the still darkened chamber shall say:

Who wakes us from the eternities of night?

The leader shall reply:

A star, a stranger, sent to bring thee light.

Some other, within, shall say:

No light of thine can raise our fallen sun,
And we are dead, because his light is gone.
Thy light as well must dim for want of breath,
Yet enter: share our darkness, and our death.

The door shall be opened, and the leader shall enter, bearing the candle. The others now say:

Thou bringest here an unfamiliar flame—
Now tell to us thine origin and name.

The leader shall answer thus:

If thou couldst see beyond the window there,
My likeness as a beacon would appear:
I live in regions far beyond thy sun—
The star thou callest **Sirius** *is my home.*

> *The great sun **Sirius!** who, though a star*
> *To thy short vision, flung from him so far,*
> *Stands sun of suns, and monarch to thy king.*
> *So by his might, he sendeth me to bring*
> *This fragment of his light, a little spark*
> *To kindle thee from sleep, and from the dark.*

Another shall say next:

> *Return upon thy wings of foreign fire,*
> *And tell thy king that we are past despair:*
> *Our bones are bare, no warmth from them may grow.*
> *We ask no gift, nor know to use one now.*

The leader shall reply:

> *But if your sun should burn and live again,*
> *Would he not raise you with him to his throne?*
> *This light I bear, though, but a candle gleam,*
> *Reveals to thee the vision I have seen:*
> *The sun is living still! Nor did he die:*
> *His strength is only hidden from this sky,*
> *But where I watch, from **Sirius'** flame,*
> *I see him burning evermore the same.*
> *None die but thee, and only by thy will*
> *Can autumn wound, and bitter winter kill.*
> *I bring thee vision, fire, and this word:*
> *That from his ashes, like a wakened bird,*
> *Shall sun leap upward, bearing on his wings*
> *The hues of every earthly bird that sings.*

Another shall then ask:

If this be so, how shall we see him rise?

The leader shall answer:

This moment, on this day, before thine eyes!

The leader shall then advance to the altar, and taking up a
handful of ashes from the basin, scatter them over the unlit
candles, after which, with the burning candle, lighting the
others. Then, setting the golden candle down before the circle of red ones, throwing back the black cloak to reveal the
red robes beneath, the leader should say this:

> *Behold now **Sirius**, sun of suns, star of thy stars,*
> *Though in my sky thou art invisible:*
> *Yet I descend in the guise of flesh, bearing truth,*
> *To succour such as ye, poor ashen creatures*
> *Sunk to madness and to sleep.*
> *Though I am cosmos to thy dust,*
> *Radiance to thy shadow, noon to the night,*
> *Still thou art the children of thy sun, and he is yet my kin,*
> *Therefore art thou flesh and blood of mine as well,*
> *And thus I give thee here my gift, my vision:*
> *Infinite sight, when thou wert doomed to blindness;*
> *Light, when thou wert dead with darkness;*
> *Wings, when thou had thought all wings unfeathered,*
> > *fallen, failed.*
> *Rise up then, children of the sun,*

Rise to his dawn, reborn,
And feathered in the colors of his infant fire:
For what was true at noon is true as well at night:
The universe is ever an immortal phoenix,
Whose death is but his birth:
Nor is the earth an exile from his breast,
Where he spreads burning wings across all space:
Where his radiance expands, there dwells all dust:
Flawed, fallen, mutable,
Yet still immortal through eternity, dying ever,
Yet no less the flesh from whence springs light:
And where the darkness ceases,
Where even one poor mote of dust
Shall flaw the sphere of silence,
There may grow some sun, some earth, and fairest life.
*And I, **Sirius**, burning eye of space, see all of these,*
And give to thine own eye all that I see.
Rise then with me,
Rise to the immortal phoenix I proclaim,
And take our radiance for thine own.

Then all shall fling aside their dark cloaks and stand revealed in equal glory. The wine shall next be poured, and all shall drink while this is said (as it once before was said at the ceremony for the Summer Solstice):

Now we shall arise,
Now we shall ascend,

Now we are assumed
In the greater fire
Of thy golden sphere,
O perfect golden king,
Never now to die,
Never to descend,
Nor to be consumed:
Now our wings are fixed
In thy heart of amber,
Now our faces fixed
In thine eye of flame,
Now our names recorded
In this single moment,
Evermore to burn
As everlasting brands
Upon the endless dark.

Then the leader, as *Sirius*, shall say:

Remember always this:
That darkness bends to light,
That death is only flight
Along the curve of space:
And every sword of ice
Is yet a crystal fair
That breaks the body's fire
To colors still more clear:
Then live redeemed from fear,

And when thou seest me
Thy winter's crystal star,
A covenant, though far
From all that we say here,
Remember how this day
I resurrect the year,
And end thy deep despair:
For flame and further flame
Break forth from all that seems
To die, but is not dead—
Though blood and flesh be shed,
By this all fires are fed.

Then the others should recite these words, spoken also at the Summer Solstice:

What is wound
About the sun
May in no way wise
Be undone;
Though the seasons
Cloud his reign,
Still we find him
Free from stain:
Fallen even
Into ruin,
He shall stand
As now we see him:

Crowned with gold,
Wreathed in joy,
Substance death
Shall not destroy.

Then shall the leader take up the gold candle, still lighted, bow to all, and go out, leaving the door open. The others may soon follow, but the twelve red candles should be left to burn down until they are consumed. So this ceremony ends, and the universal cycle is renewed.

CHARMS, SPELLS & FORMULAS

For the Making and Use of
Gris Gris Bags, Herb Candles,
Doll Magic, Incenses,
Oils and Powders

Ray Malbrough

Hoodoo magick is a blend of European techniques and the magick brought to the New World by slaves from Africa. Now you can learn the methods which have been used successfully by Hoodoo practitioners for nearly 200 years.

By using the simple materials available in nature, you can bring about the necessary changes to greatly benefit your life and that of your friends. You are given detailed instructions for making and using the "gris-gris" (charm) bags only casually or mysteriously mentioned by other writers. Malbrough not only shows how to make gris-gris bags for health, money, luck, love and protection from evil and harm, but he also explains how these charms work. He also takes you into the world of doll magick to gain love, success, or prosperity. Complete instructions are given for making the dolls and setting up the ritual.

0-87542-501-1, 192 pp., 5¼ x 8, illus., softcover $6.95

THE COMPLETE BOOK OF AMULETS & TALISMANS

Migene González-Wippler

The Pentagram, Star of David, Crucifix, rabbit's foot, painted pebble, or Hand of Fatima . . . they all provide feelings of comfort and protection, attracting good while dispelling evil.

The joy of amulets and talismans is that they can be made and used by anyone. The forces used, and the forces invoked, are all natural forces.

Spanning the world through the diverse cultures of Sumeria, Babylonia, Greece, Italy, India, Western Europe and North America, González-Wippler proves that amulets and talismans are anything but mere superstition—they are part of each man's and woman's search for spiritual connection. This book presents the entire history of these tools, their geography, and shows how anyone can create amulets and talismans to empower his or her life. Loaded with hundreds of photographs, this is the ultimate reference and how-to guide for their use.

0-87542-287-X, 304 pp., 6 x 9, photos, softcover $14.95

To order, call 1-800-THE-MOON

Prices subject to change without notice.

SPELL CRAFTS

Creating Magical Objects

*Scott Cunningham &
David Harrington*

Since early times, crafts have been intimately linked with spirituality. When a woman carefully shaped a water jar from the clay she'd gathered from a river bank, she was performing a spiritual practice. When crafts were used to create objects intended for ritual or that symbolized the Divine, the connection between the craftsperson and divinity grew more intense. Today, handcrafts can still be more than a pastime—they can be rites of power and honor; a religious ritual. After all, hands were our first magical tools.

Spell Crafts is a modern guide to creating physical objects for the attainment of specific magical goals. It is far different from magic books that explain how to use purchased magical tools. You will learn how to fashion spell brooms, weave wheat, dip candles, sculpt clay, mix herbs, bead sacred symbols and much more, for a variety of purposes. Whatever your craft, you will experience the natural process of moving energy from within yourself (or within natural objects) to create positive change.

0-87542-185-7, 224 pp., 5¼ x 8, illus., photos $10.00